The Vision of Kant

David Appelbaum gained his Ph.D. from Harvard University and his M.A. from Exeter College, Oxford. He has studied and taught philosophy for more than thirty years and is currently a professor of philosophy at State University College, New Paltz, New York. In addition to his contributions to a wide range of periodicals, his publications include the acclaimed *Everyday Spirits*, *Voice*, *Real Philosophy*, which he co-authored with Jacob Needleman, and *The Stop*. He has edited and reviewed widely and is now book review editor for *Parabola* magazine.

The Spirit of Philosophy Series

"This series of books offers the core teachings of the world's greatest philosophers, considered for the light their writings throw on the moral and material crises of our time. Repositioned in this way, philosophy and the great philosophers may once again serve humankind's eternal and ever-new need to understand who we are, why we are here, and how we are to live."

Jacob Needleman, Ph.D.
Series Editor

In the same series

The Vision of Emerson by Richard Geldard
The Vision of Wittgenstein by Henry Le Roy Finch

THE SPIRIT OF PHILOSOPHY SERIES

The Vision of Kant

Introduced and edited by
David Appelbaum

We are hindered by cleaving to time.
Whatever cleaves to time is mortal.
— MEISTER ECKHART

A catalogue record for this book is available from the British Library.

ISBN 1-84333-365-1
Printed by CPD Wales, Ebbw Vale
Cover design by Andrew Sutterby

© Vega 2001

Published in 2001 by
Vega
64 Brewery Road
London N7 9NY

Visit our website at
www.chrysalisbooks.co.uk

Permission to reproduce the following copyright material is gratefully acknowledged:
Extract from *Critique of Pure Reason*, tr. Norman Kemp Smith. London: Macmillan, 1929.
Extract from *Prolegomena to any Future Metaphysics*, tr. Peter G. Lucas. Manchester: Manchester
University Press, 1953.
Extract from *The Moral Law*, tr. H.J Paton. London: Hutchinson University Library, 1948.
Extract from *Critique of Practical Reason*, tr. Mary J. Gregor. New York: Harper and Row, 1964.
Extract for *Critique of Judgement*, tr. James Creed Meredith. Oxford: Oxford University Press, 1952.
Extract from *Religion Within the Limits of Reason Alone*, tr. Theodore M. Green and Hoyt H.
Hudson. New York: Harper and Row, 1960.

CONTENTS

PART ONE
General Introduction

Kant and the Spirit of the Modern World

The European Enlightenment of the seventeenth and eighteenth centuries was one of the great spiritual movements of modern times. It was both revolutionary and democratic, and in its peak moments, a human potential for Great Knowledge was recognized and actualized. The power of reason, not adherence to dogmatic tradition, was seen as the key to individual freedom. Blind faith and oppression by authorities of all kinds were to be replaced not merely by logic and science, but by the animation of human consciousness—reason in its fullest sense. Before humanity could know and serve its universal vision, it had to know itself.

A human and humane outlook rested on the conviction that the human mind could be perfected. Spiritual slavery—to the past, to rites and rituals, to empty devotionals—would be ended. History itself would come to an end, not by apocalypse but by overcoming itself through an inner transformation. The time was thoroughly ahistorical in its view of human nature, origin, and calling. All thinking was drawn toward a vision of the liberated self. Our present era has much in common with the Enlightenment, and as we are its spiritual children, we would do well to look closely at our parentage.

In Germany toward the end of the seventeenth century, the religious movement called "pietism" began to exert an influence. Pietism placed a strong emphasis on the experiential aspect of Christ's teachings. Justification and rebirth had to be experienced directly instead of secondhand through text and exegesis. At the same time, German deism gained an ascendance. According to deism, intellect was capable, through logic and argument, of demonstrating the existence of God and describing the nature of realms beyond the physical. Revelation, an initial stage of faith, was to be superseded by reason, the crown jewel of religious consciousness.

The young Kant, born in the university town of Königsberg in 1724, was exposed to both influences; each in its own way left an indelible impression on him. His family, though poor, was of high moral character. His father was a saddlemaker; his mother, with whom he had a strong emotional bond, died when he was fourteen. Home life fostered attitudes Kant would later place at the center of his moral universe: a sincere love of duty for its own sake, and an avoidance of hypocrisy in all matters, worldly or otherworldly.

After schooling in a local pietistic collegium, Kant at age sixteen entered the University of Königsberg, where his brilliance gained him a notoriety. Nonetheless, he turned down prestigious offers from the ministry because of his rationalistic bent and his distaste for the evangelical elements of religion. Instead, he worked as a private tutor in several homes in East Prussia. Though quiet and frail, he was thoroughly sociable. His first publication was during this period. The *General History of Nature and Theory of the Heavens* (1755) attempted to replace Newton's deistic cosmology with a purely mechanistic one. Kant wanted to render Newton's thought thoroughly consistent.

In 1770, at the age of forty-six, Kant was appointed a professor at the University of Königsberg. The appointment had been preceded by a shift in his thought. Essays in the spirit of *Observations on the Sense of the Beautiful and the Sublime* (1764) and *Dreams of a Visionary* (1766) were replaced by anti-metaphysical attitudes. The change came in part from his deeper commitment to scientific knowledge, in part from the influence of the French philosopher Jean Jacques Rousseau, who had written with deep insight on the subject of freedom. From Rousseau, Kant felt confirmed in his belief in the lawfulness of inner experience. In Rousseau's *Confessions*, the "inner man" takes precedence over outer, objective events. In spite of the pendulum swings of his thought, Kant maintained great regularity in his habits. The housewives of Königsberg set their clocks by the time he passed their windows on his afternoon walk.

Kant's inaugural dissertation, an obligatory performance upon ascending to an endowed university chair, prefigured much of his later work. Distinguishing between the world of the mind and that of the senses, he argues that the question of objectivity in knowledge can be solved only by examining the process of cognition whereby the object comes into existence. The approach was radically different from all previous attempts to explore the relation of the mind to its objects. However, the dissertation fell short in a number of areas, and, as a result, Kant was plunged for the next eleven years into a profound meditation on the mind's role in constructing reality.

Then came a decade of productivity and insight unrivaled in the modern philosophical world. In 1781, the *Critique of Pure Reason* appeared. In the preface to

the second edition, Kant refers to the reversal he under-
took in the dissertation, which now takes on proportions
of a Copernican revolution:

> Until now it was assumed that all our knowledge
> must conform or be adjusted toward objects. But
> upon this assumption all attempts to figure out *a
> priori* by concepts anything regarding such objects,
> that is, anything which would enlarge our knowl-
> edge, were failures. Therefore let us try to see
> whether we can get ahead better with the tasks of
> metaphysics if we assume that the objects should
> conform or be adjusted to our knowledge. This
> would harmonize better with the desired possibility
> of *a priori* knowledge of objects which should deter-
> mine something regarding objects prior to their
> being given to us. It is like the first thought of
> Copernicus who, when he could not get ahead with
> explaining the motions of the heavenly bodies as
> long as he assumed that the stars revolved around
> the observer, tried whether he might not be more
> successful if he let the observer revolve and allowed
> the stars to remain stationary. (B, xvi)

The *Critique* examines the cognitive limits of reason, or
"pure" reason—reason without reference to experiential
facts. Kant contrasts a legitimate use of such reason, in
mathematics, with an illegitimate one, in metaphysics,
thus freeing up the possibility of knowledge on both
sides of the boundary line.

Two years after the *Critique*, a kind of synopsis of it
appeared, entitled a *Prolegomena to any Future
Metaphysics that may be Presented as a Science*. The following year, two essays on the philosophy of history
were published: "Idea for a Universal History" and "What

is Enlightenment?" (1784). *Foundations of the Metaphysics of Morals* appeared the next year, followed, in 1788, by the *Critique of Practical Reason*, making it apparent that Kant's moral philosophy was not merely a sequel to a theory of knowledge, but an integral, original complement. For Kant, one and the same reason or consciousness finds expression in astonishingly different regions, in objective knowledge and in ethical discernment. Consciousness both discloses reality and remains subordinate to the commandments of moral action.

In both aspects, reason provides the ground for valuing individual awareness above enlightened despotism and other, not so enlightened, forms of oppression. Kant argues for an innate freedom of action, an autonomy, as he calls it. Moral choice provides a true way to the perfection and highest integration of one's human potential. At the same time, objective observation allows us to gather data about the world, social and natural, that we inhabit. Through the understanding it provides, we are more fully able to occupy our place in the cosmic scheme of things.

In 1790, the *Critique of Judgement* was published. Not as important as the first two *Critiques*, the third *Critique* investigated the idea of finality. It provided an analysis of aesthetic judgment as well as the concept of teleology in the sciences. Three years later, Kant finished *Religion Within the Limits of Reason Alone*. After its publication, he was rebuked and forbidden to write on matters of religion. In 1795 came *Eternal Peace*. Though Kant discontinued his university lectures the following year, his last major work was not published until 1797, the *Metaphysics of Morals*, one part of which dealt with justice, the other with virtue. Kant died in 1804, never having left his native city of Königsberg.

Three Questions that Changed the Face of Philosophy

What Can We Know?

An Overview

The source of Kant's thought is the experience of wonderment. Wonder reveals the twofoldness of the world to which humanity belongs. "Two things fill the mind with ever new and increasing admiration and awe," he writes,

> the oftener and more steadily we reflect on them: the starry heavens above me and the moral law within me. I do not merely conjecture them and see them as though obscured in darkness or in the transcendent region beyond my horizon: I see them before me, and I associate them directly with the consciousness of my own existence. (*Critique of Practical Reason*, 166)

Becoming aware of myself, I grow perceptive of both an outer and an inner world. Conversely, an external object or an interior event grants me awareness that I am. My existence repeatedly exclaims its wonder and wakens me to a twofold reality. Awakened, I am presented with a choice of participation.

Human nature, for Kant, is Janus-like and looks in two unbounded directions. Looking outwardly, it sees in limitless space and time and seeks to know the objects inhabiting them. Looking inwardly, it experiences unconditional freedom and strives to embody it in action. These two realms—of science and of morality—make different claims of validity and impose different burdens of responsibility on us. But their conflict is only apparent. When the consciousness (or reason, as Kant calls it) that gives rise to each is examined, their true complementarity shows itself. A second result follows from the examination. Though space and time stretch without limits, objective knowledge is in fact bounded. The boundaries allow the careful thinker to discern illusory claims of metaphysics—concerning its favorite subjects of God, the soul, and immortality—as illusory. A metaphysician's claims to know about the afterlife, divine providence, or the creation of the universe overstep the bounds of reason and practice a kind of transcendental deception. From the second result comes an important corollary: there are elements of reality that disclose themselves though a non-objectivized awareness. Moral understanding (that of a "good will") grasps truths in the very heart of our practical, everyday lives. Such truth is not susceptible to proof or disproof but must be obeyed by an obedience that predates our knowledge of our obligation.

To meet the twofoldness of the world, Kant takes up separate but complementary fields of human understanding, freedom and knowledge, duty and science. The *Critique of Pure Reason* deals with objectifying consciousness. The *Critique of Practical Reason* analyzes an immediate, conscientious awareness. The first shows how mind constructs the world as we know it, unfolding the vast universe from its own conception, and thereby having absolute responsibility in matters of science. The second shows how we participate in a moral community—how we affirm a place already given as our own—as soon as we become aware of ourselves and our destiny. Knowledge is ennobled by shining its light on the world and revealing its own creature, the object. Morality is ennobling when its inward light discloses who we are and how we are to serve our Creator. Knowledge without morality is ego-bound. Morality without knowledge is unwise.

The Background of Kant's Philosophic Revolution

A strong impetus to Kant's thinking came from the Scottish philosopher David Hume. Hume had argued that the nature of all thought is habit, or "gentle custom." Our sense organs are excited by the external world and we take in an impression that decays to an image of the object. Since any idea, however complex, is a combination of simple ideas, a science of cognition shows how all human knowledge is a habitual projection of mind. The glorious discoveries of astronomy reveal, according to Hume, no celestial truth but our own earthbound, conditional ideas. Scientific knowledge is a pipe dream since all inference and extrapolation are products of an automatic mental association. Belief, Hume wrote, "is more properly an act of the sensitive, than of the cogitative part of our nature" (*Treatise*, I.IV.1, 183). This strongly skeptical conclusion, Kant writes, "interrupted my dogmatic slumber and gave a completely different direction to my enquiries" (*Prolegomena*, 9).

When Kant awakens to his life work, he does not reject Hume's argument, but stands it on its head. In the preface to the second edition of the *Critique of Pure Reason*, he refers to the Copernican revolution in astronomy. If Copernicus removes the earth from the center of creation, Kant removes our earthly and sensorily inspired experience and makes it peripheral. He accepts the constructive role Hume had assigned to the mind, but his novel argument takes a brilliant and unexpected turn. If the mind alone is responsible for the objective world, then its knowledge—*if limited strictly to that realm*—must be absolutely trustworthy. Only when thought escapes its bounds and soars to lofty speculative regions does it run the risk of being merely associative, fantastically flawed, or delusory. Kant's creative project is to define the boundaries of valid thought, to ensure that thinking will not leave its refuge in quest of a feverish vision. Kant rhapsodizes:

> This domain is an island, enclosed by nature itself within unalterable limits. It is the land of truth— enchanting name!—surrounded by a wide and stormy ocean, the native home of illusion, where many a fog bank and many a swiftly melting iceberg give the deceptive appearance of farther shores, deluding the adventurous seafarer ever anew with empty hopes . . . (*Critique of Pure Reason* B, 295)

Kant's response to Hume's skepticism over thought is a twofold optimism. On the one hand, the human intellect has a correct field of operation within which its inferences and conclusions remain objectively valid. It is possible to study the modes of operation, learn the intellect's contribution, and even undergo nonintellectual noetic experiences (though these may not be objectively communicated). Mind makes the objective universe, and hallelujah for that! On the other hand, human intelligence surpasses the field of the intellect and is able to penetrate into a sphere of high sensitivity and awareness—the moral world. What is revealed by the cognitive mind— nature—is always subservient to what is revealed by the compassionate mind—love and respect. Knowledge illuminates the natural world, while the understanding heart illuminates the world of freedom, transforming our conditioned existence into one with real choice and responsibility. Moral understanding arises through participation, not objectivity, and is (Kant implies) the greater, deeper, and broader aspect of our human twofoldness.

A New Vision of the Human Mind and its Powers

Kant's eagerness to rescue scientific truth from Hume's skepticism is modified by his wariness of metaphysics, ontology, and speculative philosophy. Claims to know God, the soul, and immortal life are particularly suspect—and were particularly pervasive in Kant's time. The reigning philosophy was that of Christian Wolff, whose amplified version of Leibniz's rationalistic theology was orthodox thought throughout Germany. Wolff featured a great syllogistic structure with which he proved God's existence and nature. One danger of Wolff's system is to overlook the need for individual effort, insight, and revelation. That knowledge of divinity exists prior to all experience is an illusion that dissuades seekers from striving for an understanding of their own. The illusion breeds a skeptical or a dogmatic attitude toward one's search, and, as Kant says, either "is the death of sound philosophy, although the former might perhaps be entitled the euthanasia of pure reason" (*Critique of Pure Reason* B, 434). When responsibility for understanding the limits of knowledge is ignored, no understanding is possible.

Our thought has a tendency to move surreptitiously from a conditional and relative idea to one of the absolute, or a transcendental idea, in Kant's terms. With the former, one can cite evidence for or against a position, for instance, that the earth revolves around the sun. With the latter, it is impossible to decide the objective truth of the matter, for instance, that the world was created before time. Two equally defensible but opposite sides to the argument cannot be resolved. The undecidability of metaphysical debates struck Kant forcibly and led him to conclude that "the antinomies of pure reason" demonstrate the limits of sound thinking. If these limits are to be respected, the job of philosophy is to understand how the mind constructs the objective world.

The antinomies represent unfillable gaps in our mental abilities. They are the blinds spots of the mind's eye, and like the visual blind spot are quite invisible to ordinary thinking. Like the *avyakrita* that the Buddha left unanswered, they express unanswerable questions and "must be passed over in silence." Similarly, Sankara, the sage of Advaita Vedanta, utilized a dialectic of unanswerability to turn attention to what lies beyond the mind and its quest of knowledge, the Self. The antinomies themselves are four in number, having to do with (1) creation, (2) the soul, (3) freedom, and (4) an absolute being. Kant maintains that no amount of research, evidence, or theory can render our knowledge and experience objective in these matters.

The Myth and the Reality of Objectivity

From Descartes, Kant inherits the strongest focus in his search for the limits of knowledge. He follows Descartes in making a sharp distinction between sensory perception and intellectual conceptualization—although both belong to object-consciousness. Descartes writes in the *Meditations*:

> Now I have a passive power of sensation—of getting and recognizing the ideas of sensible objects. But I could never have the use of it if there were not also in existence an active power, either in myself or in something else, to produce or make the ideas. (Sixth Meditation)

While Descartes relies on God as the source of ideas, Kant places the active power in the human mind. Since the two aspects differ as passive is to active, Kant's search concerns itself almost exclusively with the process of cognition, of the intellect's coming to know an object.

Accordingly, Kant devotes great effort in the "Transcendental Aesthetic" section of the *Critique of Pure Reason* to establishing the following doctrine: "All objects of any experience possible to us are nothing but appearances, that is, mere representations which . . . have no independent existence outside our thoughts" (*Critique of Pure Reason* B, 519). Transcendental idealism (as he calls it) is a determination of the contents of ego- or object-consciousness. It specifies what can be experienced as object in our ordinary mode of awareness and adds that the object's appearance may bear no resemblance to actuality. Just as a two-dimensional perspective painting depicts three-dimensional space, so too the conceptual and perceptual artistry of the mind represents what there is. Because we lack access to reality other than through the conceptual-perceptual frame, we cannot justifiably say whether the representation is correct or accurate. There is the mind-construct, of "a something I know not what."

The realm of experience (the phenomenal world) is a product of representation. Though thought is tempted to describe the hidden face of reality (the noumenal), its real job is to render its own actions transparent to itself. This enormous effort is what the *Critique* strives to accomplish. Having seen how thought structures all possible experiences of reality, human understanding is able to take cognizance of the noumenal background in another, non-objectifying way. The discontinuities in object-consciousness point to an awareness of presences that cannot be intellectually apprehended. The "space between two thoughts" indicates a way of being and acting. In this respect, Kant's aim is like that of Buddhism's *Abhidharma*, in which clarity about the thought-construction process helps lead to liberation from thought-construction.

It would be a serious error to read Kant as denigrating nonobjective experience. To set limits to what can be objectively experienced leaves open the matter of other, nonobjective modes of apprehending the formless. The matter obviously cannot be settled by our objectifying way of knowing; or rather, to try is to embrace a dogmatic rejection of vast realms of human experience. Objective knowledge has been impressively confirmed by several hundred years of science. It cannot be dismissed and yet it is prone to presumptuously overstep its proper bounds. Once aware of the poverty of transcendental speculation—of seeking objectivity where there can be none—we can refocus on a different effort of understanding.

The Mind Alone, and the Meaning of Certainty

In formulating a reply to Hume, Kant faces a dilemma. On the one hand, he wishes to disagree with Hume regarding the constructive function of thought in order to preserve the validity of scientific conclusions. On the other he wants to agree with the mind-construction in order to eliminate dogmatic metaphysics. The way between the horns that he discovers is highly ingenious. It begins with the obvious, the form of thought itself.

Kant asks in the preface to the first edition of the *Critique*, "How much can understanding and reason know apart from all experience?" (A,xvii). He then gives the question its celebrated form: "How are synthetic *a priori* judgments possible?" The first of the two important distinctions—*a priori* [before all experience] and *a posteriori* [after experience]—separates thought that is necessary and strictly universal (i.e., without exception) from thought that is not. Mathematical equations give a good example of the former. Statements based on experience are never *a priori*. The second distinction divides thought according to whether the predicate is contained in the idea of the subject (analytic) or not (synthetic.) Kant gives the example, "All bodies are extended," as an analytic judgment because the idea of extension is part of the idea of body. It follows that every analytic judgment is *a priori*. Kant's next move is a surprise. Rather than arguing that all synthetic judgments are *a posteriori*, he goes counter to our ordinary assumptions, saying that not all synthetic judgments require empirical evidence to determine their validity.

That "natural science [physics] contains *a priori* synthetic judgments as principles" and that most of mathematics is synthetic *a priori* are both obvious to Kant (*Critique of Pure Reason* B, 17). Physical principles such as the conservation of matter or the law of action-reaction exemplify the former. That such thought exists, moreover, demonstrates the positive effect of a constructive power of mind. The mind supplies a means of organizing experimental data that predates any and all experiments. By virtue of the discovery, science is saved.

Time and Space

Everything that we see occur in the phenomenal world happens at a time and in a place. One aspect that all objects, all objective experiences, share is being spatial and temporal. There are no eternal or omnipresent *things*. Nor is there pure instantaneity nor real placelessness. Time and space seem different from other objective properties such as weight or color. Are time and space in themselves real, or are they, like other aspects of objects, constructions of the mind? The first would grant time and space absolute meaning, meaning independent of human understanding; the second, a relative one.

Kant steers a middle course similar to that concerning objectivity. Both time and space pertain to the form of experience, not its contents. Together, they comprise the frame through which perception proceeds, the lens through which we see the world. They are the "*a priori* forms of intuition," meaning that they shape sensory experience on its way to being processed into thought. Unlike other ideas, time and space are pre-cognitive. We cannot say whether time and space exist in things themselves since to put down the frame or lens and look "with naked eyes" at reality is impossible. Space and time condition a consciousness by which we, as creatures, perceive and conceive the world. They have what Kant calls a transcendental ideality. The first (space) governs the sense of the outer world; the second (time), the inner.

In the *Prolegomena*, Kant asks, "How is pure mathematics possible?" (36). Pure mathematics treats objects independently of all experience of the world. In a way, it is the exemplar of objective knowledge. The answer is that mathematicians make use of the very same "pure intuition" of space-time that frames our perceptual experience, only they do not make reference to the senses. Knowledge of sense objects is quantifiable and measurable because of this fact.

When light falls on our eyes or sound strikes our ears, the space-time frame shapes our basic receptivity to sensory experience. It is stage one of cognitive processing. Kant takes over Descartes' and Hume's idea that the body is a nullity, a strictly passive receptacle—like a window—to incoming impressions. But their entry immediately and automatically activates object-consciousness, which then goes on to assign various properties to a bare experience. In this way, perception, as contemporary cognitive scientists agree, is shot through with cognitive (or mental) elements, while concepts are custom-made for perceptual content. "Concepts without percepts are empty; percepts without concepts are blind."

The Construction of Human Experience

If perception is a prelude to the process of objectification, the succeeding stages of consciousness are equally important to clarify. In the case of perception, time and space provide the frame, or *a priori* component, in which sight, sound, smell, taste, and touch are placed. What serves a similar function in the case of cognition? Kant feels that one of the monumental discoveries of the *Critique of Pure Reason*, on a par with that of the antinomies, is the table of categories, a complete and exhaustive list of the twelve "pure concepts of the understanding."

Giving these concepts subheads of quantity, quality, relation, and modality (and freely adopting them from
Aristotle's categories in the *Metaphysics*), Kant contends
that the concepts collectively ensure that (1) experience
possesses a necessary cognitive unity (rather than, à la
Hume, one stemming from habit and accident), and (2)
the meaning is not private, but capable of being understood by everyone. He also argues that their objective
validity "as *a priori* concepts rests, therefore, on the fact
that so far as the form of thought is concerned, through
them alone does experience become possible" (B, 126).

The material given in an unknowable form is initial-
ly filtered through the pure intuition and then acted upon
by the higher concepts, whose special elevation indicates
a greater universality and power of unifying diverse
strands of consciousness. Their action (the *thinking* of
thought) is not part of ordinary awareness since our
focus is by training on their results (the thought itself.) As
our awareness of the processing deepens, a new problem in objectification appears. How can concepts that do
not originate in experience apply to experience? The
interfacing faculty is the schematism, which takes a sensory image, gleaned from an encounter with an object
and subject to a spatio-temporal awareness, and relates it
to higher categories that lack such awareness. Working
with the textures and tones of the image, the schematism
brings the process to recognition, whereupon we
exclaim, "It's a tree!"

To each of the four categories of "pure" concepts
correspond principles that determine broad aspects of
object-consciousness. To quantity, quality, relation, and
modality correspond axioms of intuition, anticipations of
perception, analogies of experience, and postulates of
empirical thought. Each aspect imparts its specific flavor

to awareness of the object. For instance, under analogies of experience, we find the idea of a permanent substance that underlies constant phenomenal change, and the idea of causation that out of necessity binds temporally diverse objects together.

Who Experiences?

A striking feature of everyday experience of things is that it seems to belong to one and the same subject, I myself. Is the wholeness of consciousness conferred by the conceptual and perceptual frame sufficient to guarantee this unity? For Kant, it is not.

> There can be in us no items of knowledge, no connection or unity of one item of knowledge with another, without that unity of consciousness which precedes all data of intuitions, and by relation to which representations of objects are alone possible. This pure original unchangeable consciousness I shall name *transcendental apperception.* (*Critique of Pure Reason* A, 107)

Put simply, if there is an awareness of an object, it is my (or your) awareness. Objective knowledge always belongs to someone whose awareness it is.

In a way, Kant agrees with Hume on the issue of personal identity; in another, he disagrees. Hume flatly denied a real basis to a continuing self of experience. The transcendental unity of apperception is not, however, a sense of self occasioned by experience. The experiential or psychophysical self is itself a product of the process of objectification. By the same token, one cannot become aware of the apperceiving self since that would be to objectify it. Kant is speaking of the form, not the content, of object-consciousness, of its design, not what it contains. The "representation 'I' [is] simple and in itself completely empty" (*Critique of Pure Reason* B, 404). Such an 'I' stipulates a condition for awareness of the realm of forms but no specific form whatsoever.

> It must be possible for the "I think" to accompany all my representations; for otherwise something would be represented in me which could not be thought at all, and that is equivalent to saying that the representation would be impossible, or at least would be nothing to me. (*Critique of Pure Reason* B, 131-132)

Still, Kant may waver between two notions. Can we become aware of the transcendental unity of apperception, given that such awareness is not of an object? If the 'I' is only a formal or logical requirement of object-consciousness, the answer is negative. But Kant also says that "in the synthetical original unity of apperception, I am conscious of myself, not as I appear to myself, nor as I am in myself, but [I am conscious] only that I am" (*Critique of Pure Reason* B, 157). An immediate, direct, and unprocessed awareness—of a sort Kant does not examine—would apparently open to an impression of one's own existence. Participation in the mystery of existence yields data relating the psychophysical self to the formless realm that Buddhists and Vedantists call Self.

The Dream of Things in Themselves

Kant offers the intriguing suggestion that beyond the representation of the object, constructed by ego-consciousness, lies its unconstructed, nonrepresentational counterpart, the thing in itself. In his own terms, we cannot *say* anything about things in themselves, cannot even mention their existence, since language itself is an objectifying activity. They are "there," like the vanishing point of a perspective drawing, barely thinkable. Nor can we *not* think them since

> we must yet be in a position at least to *think* them as things in themselves; otherwise we should be landed in the absurd conclusion that there can be appearance without anything that appears. (*Critique of Pure Reason* B, xxvi)

Is it absurd to think, along with the Yogacara school of Buddhism or Berkeley's idealism, that there is consciousness in the midst of its constructive activity, period? That nothing exists but consciousness? Kant vigorously assumes that reality exists independently of mind, though notwithstanding his doctrine is called "transcendental idealism." To speak of the thing in itself as the transcendental object is to reveal the mind's impulse to shape the formless and unknowable. Kant seems pressed even to explain this idea:

> By that is meant a something = x, of which we know, and with the present constitution of our understanding can know, nothing whatsoever, but which, as a correlate of the unity of apperception, can serve only for the unity of the manifold in sensible intuition. (*Critique of Pure Reason* A, 250)

In the end, Kant proposes the notion of a noumenon to mark thought's tendency to hyperextend itself. A noumenon is not an ordinary concept (like "body" or "speed") belonging to object-consciousness, but one of a rare class designed to regulate the operation of object-consciousness. Its function is negative, "to prevent intuition from being extended to things in themselves, and thus to limit the objective validity of sensible knowledge"

(*Critique of Pure Reason* B, 310). Curbing the pretension of the ego, noumena preserve a realm of consciousness for the exclusive operation of duty and morality.

Destroying the "Science of Being"

Having gained clarity about the noumenal realm, Kant realizes his double aim of protecting science while destroying ontology. Ontology, as dogmatic metaphysics, professes objective knowledge of things in themselves. It erroneously projects the frame of conditionality onto the unconditional and draws relative conclusions about the absolute. Kant divides the field of ontology into three headings : doctrine of the soul, cosmology, and knowledge of God. They parallel precisely the topics studied in the antinomies of pure reason.

Textbooks on the soul—or rational psychology—were as prevalent in Kant's day as in our own. Leibniz, their immediate progenitor, derives the soul's relation to levels of existence above and below the sensory through an analysis of the idea of indivisibility. Descartes determines the body's relation to consciousness in an analogous, *a priori* way. Lesser thinkers made more extravagant claims, purporting to chart the soul's career before birth and after death. For Kant, such projects derive, as he says, from a "single text": the "I think," or unity of apperception. We have already noted the tendency to take the "I think" as a specific content rather than as the form of ego- or object-consciousness in general. When a doctrine of the soul is plagued by this false premise, a scientific psychology (Kant's desideratum) is precluded. Only collecting data on an empirical or psychophysical self can render a study of soul objective.

Similar considerations apply to the idea of cosmology, the well-ordered totality of totalities. The legitimate operation of object-consciousness is to synthesize and unify the divergent strands of raw experience, render all experience holistic. To objectify the synthesizing activity itself, however, is to exceed the limits established for sound thinking. It is to substitute the correct and negative use of cosmology—to *regulate* concepts—with an erroneous and positive use—to *constitute* concepts.

The idea of God or the absolute involves a parallel hyperextension of thought, in this case, the idea of the sum of all possibilities. To make an object of God is to confuse a condition of thought in itself with a particular content of cognitive activity. It is to use a transcendental or pure concept in the domain of ordinary experience— as if the context of an idea has no bearing on its application. Kant goes on to dispose of three traditional arguments for the existence of God: (1) the Ontological Proof that says God exists in reality because we think and predicate existence of Him; (2) the First Cause Proof that says God exists, or else there would be an infinite causal series to explain events; and (3) the Argument from Design that says the structure of creation itself proves the existence of a Creator.

The negative arguments notwithstanding, Kant believes in the legitimacy of religion. The delicate tissue of individual experience must be protected from the brusque attacks of abstract thought. Spiritual practice is not devoted to a concept or fact, but to the immediacy of experience. Present, noncomparative awareness brings the unprocessed contents of the moment into the light. Such awareness, for Kant, belongs to a person engaged in moral agency, in a search for the ultimate ground of duty. The possibility of religion, therefore, rests in clearing the ground of morality, and we must postpone discussion until that point.

What Should We Do?

The Meaning of Ethics

Human knowledge is fallen knowledge. It is barred from entry into the unconditional realm, stopped short by its imperative to hold to a representation of reality. Representation reduplicates in thought and concept what abides in itself, ever-changing, unimpeded by the human need for control. Objective knowledge freezes a dynamic play of forces, creating a form whose permanence can be grasped and preserved. Objectivity therefore implies distance, disengagement, and direction—the cost of which is confinement of thought to the realm of relativity. Little does the mind make note of its prison when the profit is mastery over the physical world. So goes the story that we children of the absolute sell our birthright for a bowl of pottage.

Any question about our participation in the unconditional, formless reality must come by virtue of an immediate, present awareness. Objectivity, with its continuous glance back to a fixed conceptual frame, relies on the past for a basis of knowledge. Analysis, explanation, and theorization must be dropped before we can be subject of the other realm. We must, in short, let drop the ego and its mode of consciousness and enter into an awareness that, by not separating us from the world, preserves our community with a wider realm of being.

An awareness of unconditionality leaves us duty-bound to serve it if we wish to express that aspect of our twofold nature. What we experience as duty—an obligation to act independent of the dictates of the ego—is the unconditional realm manifesting through our agency. When we obey the unconditional imperative or "the moral law," as Kant calls it, we cease to be subject to the conditions and limitations imposed by the objectification process. Since it is nature or the natural world that is mind-constructed, obedience to the moral law grants us freedom from nature—the nature of ego and the nature of causation. The development of moral consciousness is, for Kant, the way to liberation. Since liberation alone brings real choice—not mere automatic decision-making by inclination or desire—self-realization follows its pathway.

Kant follows Aristotle in distinguishing a practical (or action-based) from a theoretical (or reflective) use of human reason. Kant is comfortable with Aristotle's subsequent division of human excellence into moral and intellectual virtue. For Kant, but not for Aristotle, however, moral virtue reigns supreme. Kant notes that reason's "true function must be to produce a *will* which is *good*, not as a *means* to some further end, but *in itself*" (*The Moral Law*, 7). Moral awareness opens us to a destiny that remains an unprovable idea to the intellect. Without moral awareness, ethics is a form of compulsion, the tyranny of "You should," "You ought not," "You are supposed to." It is an ethics of guilt and resentment, not love and respect.

Freedom and Human Destiny

The third antinomy of the first *Critique* is a reminder that freedom as an *idea* is without value. To determine whether freedom or complete causal necessity governs the world is impossible by intellectual means alone. Kant repeats this conclusion in the *Critique of Practical Reason*: "Speculative reason could think of freedom without contradiction, but it could not assure any objective reality to it" (3). In addition, only a negative idea of freedom is derived by this route: a free will is one not made to act by causes alien to it such as another person's threats, hypnotic suggestion, or the passion of the moment. Is there a more substantial, positive aspect of freedom?

Kant is lucid about the difference between freedom and license. No distinction is more integral to a working moral understanding. Being free, far from allowing us to do whatever we may want, constrains action and renders us ever more obedient to lawfulness. Law does not, however, return us to the karmic folds. The two sides of our nature face different orders of law. On one side, nature and her laws bind us to the dictates of appetite and mortality, reactivity and craving. On the other, our own inner composition, peculiar to being human, searches for its specific destiny. The first direction is necessitated by our position in a cosmos governed by natural laws. The second is prompted solely by a moral aspiration to respond to the call of our being. The essence of who we are—as "rational beings," in Kant's terms—is to embody autonomy, "the property which will has of being a law to itself" (*The Moral Law,* 98). In a paradoxical manner, freedom involves a shift from lawfulness to lawfulness, from a neutralization of a set of laws that diminish us to an embrace of another set that lets us be free.

The agenda of the intellect, "pure reason," is to construct the world of ego-consciousness. The image of causal reality, however, ultimately discloses the lever by which the ego controls its world: the concept of cause itself. To relinquish the agenda is to be receptive to an awareness of a more central core. Passing from law unto law, we become who we are, unimpeded by alien influences in the task of expressing ourselves through practical reason. Setting aside the objective world, we take our place unknowingly, through the practice of an unconditional obedience to laws of freedom.

The Power of Reason

The primary project of the *Critique of Practical Reason* is "merely to show that there is a pure practical reason" (3). It is a monumental undertaking. That consciousness is in itself an action, and not simply a something we use to think with, is a novel idea. It changes the meaning of consciousness, suggesting that consciousness acts directly, in-forming us with its intelligence, and transforming what is fixed and stagnant into what is alive and present.

Kant alludes to the dynamic luminance in *The Moral Law* when he describes will as a "consciousness of . . . causality in regard to actions," and further as a "consciousness of a law of action" (102). The throes of making a practical decision may bring about a stop in the headlong speed of ego-consciousness. We ask, "What should be done?" Often enough, we face a conflict between competing desires. In the midst of the quandary, an opening to another consciousness may occur. Kant describes the inner situation in precise terms:

> It is therefore the moral law, of which we become immediately conscious as soon as we construct maxims for the will, which first presents itself to us; and, since reason exhibits it as a ground of determination which is completely independent of and not to be outweighted by any sensuous condition, it is the moral law which leads directly to the concept of freedom. (*Critique of Practical Reason*, 29–30)

An immediate awareness of the unconditional realm (a "pure spontaneity") reminds us of ourselves—not in the guise of psychosocial entities but as rational beings. We are called to conduct our lives accordingly. Kant calls present awareness and its startling effect on how we are, a "fact of reason" and "the sole fact of pure reason" (*Critique of Practical Reason*, 31). The terminology may seem contradictory since facts belong to the world of objective experience. So strikingly factual is the disclosure of inner becoming that Kant wishes to set off this moment of consciousness from all else.

To be impressed by the fact of reason is to strive for freedom. Specific conditions differ from situation to situation, but in all cases the same openness to the unconditional realm dictates a course of free action. We are thereby receptive to a categorical imperative, the specific form that the moral law takes. "Categorical" means not conditioned by exceptions, extenuations, or provisos, while "imperative" means that we are ordained by our being to obey. The fundamental experience of freedom wells up from the depths of our being and constrains our action in the face of other, superficial impulses.

The Self Alone and Free

Of our twofoldness and the two directions that invite our attention, Kant writes that one

> can consider himself first—so far as he belongs to the sensible world—to be under laws of nature (heteronomy); and secondly—so far as he belongs to the intelligible world—to be under laws which, being independent of nature, are not empirical but have their ground in reason alone. (*The Moral Law*, 109)

That laws of nature are heteronomous (*hetero*-, other than, plus *nomos*, law) means that inclination, craving, and desire, which compete as motives for action, originate outside our being. It also means that elements of ego-consciousness cannot qualify as nonheteronomous, or autonomous (*auto-*, self), impulses of the will. Only action undertaken to conform with an unconditional demand meets the measure of autonomy. We give the law to ourselves only when action ceases to spring from natural causes, from the ego's natural tendency to seek the object of desire.

When is a demand of unconditionality actually felt? Is there a way to specify the gap in ego-consciousness through which comes an awareness of the other aspect? The paradigm context arises when duty conflicts with desire, though it is safe to say that this is not the sole context. When, however, what we want and what we ought to do—for the sake of ourselves—pull in different directions, the condition for a temporary cessation of ego-consciousness may obtain. It is misleading to summarize the condition, as often is done, as "duty for duty's sake." Kant is examining a kind of renunciation in which we let go of private interest for the sake of a wider vision of ourselves and reality. To let go of private goals (given as a hypothetical imperative) is to serve a goal common to everyone, an end in itself (a categorical imperative).

An unconditional awareness, insofar as it comes into contact with ordinary life, is a reminder of spiritual growth and inner freedom. It comes at its own time and bidding, though a difficult or perilous choice seems to call it forth. The task is to cultivate a receptivity to it. Kant recommends two different approaches, each involving its own formulation of a principle that engenders moral consciousness: universal law and the end in itself.

The principle of universal law, as an expression of the categorical imperative, has the makeup of a logical rule. It says, "So act that the maxim of your will could always hold at the same time as a principle establishing universal law" (*Critique of Practical Reason*, 30). Kant's basic point is simple. If one's choice of action also could be undertaken by everyone, then we can presume the person has renounced all private ends or interests—all that marks one out as a special, particular instance. It is not difficult, moreover, to determine whether a choice could be universal law. Take a choice and find out whether a contradiction results if everyone were to act on it. If someone is, for instance, trying to decide whether to suicide, the act, if universalized, would involve an inconsistency of sorts. As Kant notes, "A system of nature by whose law the very same feeling whose function is to stimulate the furtherance of life should actually destroy life would contradict itself" (*The Moral Law*, 53). Suicide is thereby precluded as a morally acceptable act.

There is a tendency in Kant's thought to construe the principle of universal law in narrow terms, as if it provided the moral equivalent of the logical law of non-contradiction. In another example, a person who borrowed money considers defaulting on the loan. Asking what would happen if all borrowers acted similarly, leads to the discovery that the institution of promising would collapse. That conclusion suffices to convince him or her of the moral error of this choice. At best, however, the exercise of universalization furnishes a gauge for an unconditional awareness. Its virtue lies in creating a stop, in which the ego may move aside and allow space for an enlarged awareness. Its danger is that it may become a mechanical test, a contrivance whose real purpose is lost in the objective computation it gives. In such a case, natural laws and egoistic calculations once again have sway.

The second formulation of a principle expressing the unconditional is that of the end in itself. It is a principle of categorical respect.

> Act in such a way that you always treat humanity,
> whether in your own person or in the person of any
> other, never simply as a means, but always at the
> same time as an end. (*The Moral Law*, 66)

An end in itself is a source of absolute value. We recognize such value, not by a market price, but by its manifest presence and dignity. To deny the valuation, in oneself or in another, is to remain unbecoming as a person. It is to refuse the call to be free both *from* that which diminishes humanity and *toward* that which enlarges one's human nature. "There are in humanity," Kant observes, "capacities for greater perfection which form part of nature's purpose for humanity in our person" (*The Moral Law*, 70). The development of consciousness in its breadth, depth, and height is the chief means of fulfilling our promise as human beings. An effort in this direction, moreover, carries us farther than speculative reason can, since "when this respect has become active and dominating, it allows us a view into the realm of the supersensuous, though only a glimpse" (*Critique of Practical Reason*, 148).

Conversely, growth is not served as long as self-love instruments choice. Limited, heteronomous goals stem from a dimmed awareness of the higher purpose to which Kant refers. Lack of respect—in actuality, a clouded moral vision—devalues the perpetrator more than the victim. Yet, such a refusal too has an indirect, positive effect on a search for goodness since a distaste for one's self-conceit can awaken feeling for the moral law. Furthermore, an act of making the other an object closes one to the transformatory action of a finer moral consciousness and leaves one cut off from humanity and from the community of rational beings to which humanity belongs. Kant gives a romantic description of a "kingdom of ends" to this community:

> We shall be able—if we abstract from the personal difference between rational beings, and also from all the content of their private ends—to conceive a whole of all ends in systematic conjunction . . . (*The Moral Law*, 74)

In the vision, we are each related to one another by virtue of participation in an integrated whole (a cosmos). As long as we do not stray from the relation—upheld through an awareness of the unconditional—we do our part in maintaining the created universe.

Reading Kant's moral thought may leave us feeling that ethics is an isolating, lonely affair that requires a rigor to stand apart from passions and pleasures that otherwise "make us human." Nothing could be farther from the truth. Inclination, feeling, desire—the masks of the ego—unavoidably estrange us from a deeper relation with ourselves and others. Nourished by such a relation, we are enabled to develop a range of human capacities that otherwise atrophy. Deprived of it, we turn to violence, practiced first against the self, then against the other. Only by penetrating and being penetrated by an active awareness of the unconditional can we live lives of felt community. Duty alone—when understood as liberation from oppressive self-love—can break down the prison walls of the ego.

In this vein, we can listen to Kant's paean to duty:

> Duty! Thou sublime and mighty name that doest embrace nothing charming or insinuating but requirest submission and yet seekest not to move the will by threatening aught that would arouse

natural aversion or terror, but only holdest forth a
law which of itself finds entrance into the mind and
yet gains reluctant reverence (though not always
obedience)—a law before which all inclinations are
dumb even though they secretly work against it:
what origin is there worthy of thee, and where is to
be found the root of thy noble descent which
proudly rejects all kinship with the inclinations and
from which to be descended is the indispensable
condition of the only worth which men can give
themselves? (*Critique of Practical Reason*, 86)

Laws of Freedom

Kant's intent is to establish morality on an *a priori*
basis. He means that the incentive for moral action must
arise from beyond ego- or object-consciousness. An
"independence from sensuous impulse in the determination of choice" requires a motive other than desire, feeling, inclination, or pleasure (*The Doctrine of Virtue*, 212).
Kant's ethical thought stands on an entirely different foot-
ing than Hume's. Hume develops an ethics based on the
feeling of sympathy, that is, an empirical ethics. Similar
approaches exist in eudaemonism, hedonism, and utili-
tarianism, all of which regard pleasure or happiness as
motivation for moral action. Each allows choice to be
determined by egoistic interest rather than by an awareness of what is common to all beings. Yet when all is
said and done, a great mystery remains concerning why
one acts in accordance with the moral law. Kant asks:

On what do we base the worth we attach to this way
of acting—a worth supposed to be so great that there
cannot be any interest which is higher? And how
does it come about that in this alone man believes

himself to feel his own personal worth, in comparison with which that of a pleasurable or painful state
is to count as nothing? (*The Moral Law*, 102)

The questions return us to the intimacy of spiritual commitment. The call to liberation and our response to it are
the dark, fertile ground of inner determination. Proof that
an undeniable wish to be free guides action and that the
wish is a lawful sign of our twofold nature is required of
each person. Those able to testify through word and
deed show themselves already cognizant of the value of
a moral life.

Toward a Definition of Virtue

Kant paints very broad strokes on the canvas in his
early moral thought. Occupied with problems left over
from the first *Critique*, he examines the main implications
of our dual commitment: objectivity and unconditionality.
He describes in general terms the twin cornerstones of
his ethical theory: the nature of categorical obligation
and the source of value. Then, he sketches an account of
how universal principles affect the choice of specific
actions. We are left with a foundation and frame, lumi-
nous with new discoveries.

If Kant's work ended here, we would be left to pon-
der how to apply its considerable insight in daily life. To
an astonishing degree, Kant was able, in the latter part of
his career, to fill in details of his moral scheme and to
systematize his thinking. The mature work is entitled *The
Metaphysics of Morals* and has two parts, *The Doctrine of
Law* and *The Doctrine of Virtue*. The second develops
material given in the early *Lectures on Ethics* and is relevant to the present study.

Kant takes the Aristotelean notion of virtue as a

human excellence and turns it in the direction of our inner commitments. Virtue is not simply a way of behaving but an attitude that springs into action. A virtuous attitude differs from those deriving from pleasure-seeking and avoidance of pain that one habitually brings to life. Virtue is consciously formed and continuously reformed. Whenever the attitude grows encrusted with habit, it must be formed anew. Since it arises only in opposition to habit—as it were in the stop between moments of habitual reaction—Kant considers virtue to be "self-constraint according to a principle of inner freedom" (*The Doctrine of Virtue*, 393). A finer, more active awareness freed from egoistic machinations awakens us to our true purpose. Reminded of our origin and destiny, we relinquish control and willingly serve the needs of the present situation. Virtue lies in this direction.

Inner composure is, therefore, an ingredient of a virtuous attitude. Kant uses the word "apathy" in an obsolete definition to denote the freedom from emotional agitation required of a receptive moral awareness. Reverence for the moral law is possible only when the way is no longer blocked by compulsive desires of our nature. Kant, however, does not urge a rigoristic approach or a nagging conscience. "Fantastic virtue," he warns, "is a micrology which, were it admitted into the doctrine of virtue, would turn the sovereignty of virtue into a tyranny" (*The Doctrine of Virtue*, 408).

To clear Kant of the charges of rigorism is to notice a latitude in his formulation of ethics. Some virtuous duties follow the form of juridical duties, which are of narrow obligation and admit no exception. Many duties of virtue, however, are of wide obligation and allow room to play in meeting them. They are imperfect in the sense that they prescribe broad policies, trends of behavior, or courses of action, rather than specific acts. They call for the use of discretionary judgment. The imperfect duty of not lying to oneself, for instance, demands an attentiveness to what one really means to say. Forgetfulness on any one occasion does not imply an immorality. Instead, it measures how finely developed a moral awareness is in operation. Perfect virtue is the work of saints and supererogation. Though necessary to the scale of virtuous behavior (in locating moral perfection), it is not required of anybody. Kant observes that "the closer to narrow duty [one] brings the maxim of observing this duty (in his attitude of will), so much the more perfect is his virtuous action" (*The Doctrine of Virtue*, 389).

Two general policies of virtue are dictated by a search for moral consciousness: one's own perfection and the happiness of others. The substantive policies falling under each heading are traditional exemplars of vice and virtue. One might find similar choices, for instance, in Augustine and Dante. However, the arrangement is peculiar to Kant. The happiness of others involves duties of love (wide duties), including beneficence, gratitude, and sympathy, as well as duties of respect (narrow duties), including pride, calumny, and mockery. The latter are exceptionless while the former require a discerning eye for their application. Further evidence of room to play is found in the moral weight of an omission of each. "To neglect mere duties of love is *lack of virtue* (*peccatum*). But to neglect duty that proceeds from the *respect* due to every man as such is *vice* (*vitium*)" (*The Doctrine of Virtue*, 463).

In the case of one's own perfection, the division is somewhat different. Bearing in mind the twofold character of human life, we look to both to the natural and the moral, and possess two types of perfectibility. As a member of the natural world, we are obligated in a strict or narrow sense not to suicide, and to avoid sexual self-defilement, overindulgence, and intemperance. As a member of the kingdom of ends, we are under wide obligation to avoid lying, avarice, and false humility. Kant's designations may reflect mores that are dated or quaint, but even if this assessment is sound, it does not affect his deep insights into moral awareness. Their validity continues regardless of specific moral policies of choice.

The Dynamics of Human Transformation

The architectonic majesty of Kant's moral thought is most visible and most visibly appreciated. Examining powerful principles, it reaches toward an understanding of the core concepts of ethics. It conveys the impression of a monument, impassive to time's march, fixed and enduring. There is, however, a concealed dimension, much more hidden: a dynamic of self-transformation. Ethics, for Kant, is a means, *the* sole means, of striving to attain perfection. It embodies a way of understanding, a new mode of consciousness that requires the cooperation of intellect, feeling, and body. It expresses itself through action, and since inaction is not a human option, it is expressed willy-nilly, regardless of what we do. To be able to act in accordance with the moral law is to be enlightened by an intelligence deep within the human soul that far surpasses that of intellect. Growth of this ableness is precisely the way to an understanding heart.

To strive toward perfection is obligatory. To cultivate awareness of freedom is to lead a virtuous life. Virtue is its own reward since its illumined radiance, like the *satchit* of Vedanta, is blissful.

Perfection, Kant reminds us, is also twofold. There is perfection of natural talents, aptitudes, and capabilities such as athletic prowess or mathematical acumen. To help complete what nature has begun, one ought to strive to develop such potentials. More essential to the point, there is perfection of the moral dimension in humanity. Cultivation of this dimension involves what Kant calls duty "from a motive of duty." The practice involves a conscious turning away from objectifications of the ego and toward a relationship with the unconditional. The specificity of categorical demands does not always correspond to a list of duties. An act of moral intelligence (casuistry, in Kant's sense) is required to translate the unconditional demand into the language of the conditional.

To nurture both the courage to meet the unconditional and the resourcefulness to act under its gaze is to seek the "moral motive." Since to renounce all egoistic striving is at the same time to open to a higher consciousness, the "moral motive" is a call to service. To become a part of a "kingdom" of beings responsible for the maintenance of the creative universe requires persistent and unceasing effort. The attainment is endless since "if the practice of virtue were to become habit the agent would suffer loss to the *freedom* in adopting maxims which characterize an action done from duty" (*The Doctrine of Virtue*, 408). Nonetheless, as more of one's being accepts the task, one incrementally approaches a full embodiment of virtue. One becomes a human being and, becoming human, takes the place allotted humans in the lineage of the absolute.

In the end, a subtle error of defeatism must be avoided. When our moral destiny is thought to lie beyond the bounds of attainment, we risk an impotent

striving. The error degrades in one swoop the moral law
and our own inner strength of will. We indulge ourselves
in what Kant calls "fanatical theosophical dreams" and
reject the experience of self-knowledge. The nature of
twofoldness peculiar to humanity bridges the gulf
between absolute and relative, categorical and hypothetical, and autonomous and heteronomous. Unless we are
wholeheartedly committed to work for perfection, in the
full sense of the word, we are in denial of this nature.
That we meet what hinders progress is a measure of
commitment. We meet it and move on. As Kant puts it,

> We are only hindered in the unceasing striving
> toward the precise and persistent obedience to a
> command of reason which is stern, unindulgent,
> truly commanding, really and not just ideally possi-
> ble. (*Critique of Practical Reason*, 123)

What Can We Hope For?

Religion and the Spirit

The holy and the sacred are not absent from Kant's
moral philosophy. Contact with an unconditional and
mysterious presence is fraught with the perils of both,
and to the extent that we strive toward inwardness, we
lead a life of spirit. Since religion, in its root meaning,
has to do with strict observance, Kantian ethics draws its
nourishment from the deep stratum of religious experience. Here, the source of hope (together with that of
love and faith) is concealed. Hope has its opposite of
despair, which arises with disengagement, slackness, and
non-effort. Hope, therefore, has to do with an understanding of moral and spiritual perfection. It accepts the
fact that human striving is an absolutely essential ingredi-

ent in the evolution of awareness. The act of striving, rather than an intellectual comprehension of it, animates the will to become whole, and, in this becoming, embodies a consciousness of the noumenal realm.

Though too summary, the notion that religion is concerned with God, the soul, and immortality is not inexact. Our hope is to enliven the aspect of ourselves that serves an absolute being in a timeless, eternal fashion. Taken as concepts in the frame of the object world, the three ideas are meaningless. Kant demonstrates this fact, we saw, with the antinomies of the first *Critique*. They are, however, transubstantiated in the course of a striving for a moral awareness of our place, our holy, human place. Through a struggle to be receptive to an unconditional demand, we are granted a heartfelt, nonintellectual understanding of God's existence and the soul's immortal being. This amounts to embracing a "pure practical faith." The teaching guides us toward (echoing Meister Eckhart) a disinterested respect. In the course of its practice, the faithful may righteously proclaim:

> I will that there be a God, that my existence in this world be also an existence in a pure world of the understanding outside the system of natural connections, and finally that my duration be endless. (*Critique of Practical Reason*, 143)

Religion and the Moral Imperative

Religion in Kant's day (and our own) was generally taken to mean revealed religion, a religion of rites and dogmas. "Except ye see signs and wonders, ye will not believe" (John 4:48). Belief in miracles and the authority of scripture is a mark of the Abrahamic faiths, especially Christianity. Revealed religions demand a humiliation of reason as such, and are barren ground for the nurturing of spiritual awareness. Reacting strongly against this position, Kant proposes a new conception of religion, explored in *Religion Within the Limits of Reason Alone*. Its act of fidelity lies "in the heart's disposition to fulfil all human duties as divine commands" (*Religion*, 79). It is a supremely moral religion. Because it tended to debunk the then current practice of Christianity, Kant was asked by King Frederick William II of Prussia to desist from further writing on religion. His compliance was ambiguous.

The divine—that is, the unconditional as attributed to a single Being—cannot be an object of thought. That phenomenal experience never provides material to fill out a concept of God has already been established in the first and second *Critiques*. Absolute being, however, can function as a regulatory, rather than a constitutive, idea. Its very emptiness serves to indicate what lies behind the conceptual frame. Like a finger pointing to the moon, it beckons the observer to look beyond the gesture of representation. To regard one's duty as unconditionally commanded is to look in this direction. One acts *as if* one had knowledge that the command were divinely issued, even though such knowledge is impossible. Action *as if* has the form of divine service since it embodies an awareness of the sacred origin of all action. It can be compared to Krishna's teaching of yoga in the *Bhagavad Gita*:

> Abandoning attachment to fruits
> of action, always content, independent,
> he does nothing at all
> even when he engages in action.
>   (4:20, Miller translation)

Moral religion—to act *as if* duty were divinely commanded—answers a definite inner need. To allow room for the unconditional requires a wholehearted commitment. "Purity of heart" (in Kierkegaard's terms), single-mindedness, or emptiness alone gives entry to a consciousness of the way. Attachments dropped, one becomes a disinterested participant in the working of a higher force that guides one's intention. *What* is at work cannot be grasped as an object. In a noncognitive fashion, however, recognition of that to which one's will submits is possible. Moral religion bends its knee to the source of that recognition and pays homage to all things that adore it.

Good and Evil Re-Defined

Religion, moral or otherwise, must grapple with the problem of evil. That "the world lieth in evil" (1 John 5:19) ever since the passing of a Golden Age or Edenic epoch is an idea diffused into many, many traditional religions. Concerning such evil, what is its nature, and origin, and what is the possibility of eradicating it?

The locus of the problem is found in our relations with other people. Harm may be intentionally inflicted or goodness intentionally scorned. Religious thought must, therefore, determine whether an impulse to do evil exists or whether the act is a temporary lapse in doing good. Put another way, can one freely make up one's mind to do something wrong, or is wrong-doing a forgetfulness of one's freedom?

In this regard, Kant adapts Plato's idea that the good is an absolute that has no opposite. "It is impossible," he boldly claims, "to conceive anything at all in the world, or even out of it, which can be taken as good without qualification, except a *good will*" (*The Moral Law*, 1). The will's goodness consists solely in being responsive to the summons of the unconditional insofar as it contacts humanity. Its value lies in providing the ground for a higher, moral awareness and not in any particular action it prompts. Even if it could do nothing, Kant rhapsodizes, "even then it would still shine like a jewel for its own sake as something which has its full value in itself" (*The Moral Law*, 3).

To speak of a good will may sound quaint, but the idea has acute importance. What Kant has in mind is as far from desire as awareness is from thought. Will is more akin to a willingness to witness the principle of freedom in oneself than to a trying-to-do. The ever-changing, unknowable realm of the unconditional is constantly at work. At the same time, in order for it fully to manifest, our assent is needed. Acknowledged by human consciousness, the moral law is granted passage into the phenomenal world. Our role as conscious ("rational") beings is fulfilled by the single act of presence. The act is none other than a good will shining forth.

An act that involves a simultaneous acknowledgment of one's freedom has a palpably different quality. It is not authorized solely by the ego. Desire for the object is not its motive. Expressive up to a degree of an inner presence, the act partially communicates one's categorical obligations. The impact of a selfless deed testifies to the fact that reverence for the unconditional is a felt value, and that "reverence is the assessment of a worth which far outweighs all the worth of what is commended by inclination" (*The Moral Law*, 20). That we are equipped to recognize the difference that moral awareness makes in our lives is the central point of Kant's moral religion.

That will is a responsiveness, freely given, to absolute commands of the noumenal realm clarifies the question of evil. Kant takes up a complex position with regard to human responsibility. When no obstacle impedes the goodness of the will, one is able to take responsibility, inward as well as outward. When expression of moral worth is blocked—due to a habit of egoistic gratification—the awareness necessary for responsible action is missing. This is the doctrine of responsibility in its absolute sense. Yet still, the action, whether petty or profoundly global, does not escape assessment of moral worth. It is wrong, misguided, imprudent, or poorly chosen if the agent's disposition is not to evil-doing. But it is evil per se if the person has made it a policy to do so. This is a relative responsibility.

The distinction between absolute and relative responsibility modifies the simplicity of Kant's thought about will. The will to moral awareness, he tells us, is either impeded or unimpeded. The willingness that manifests a good will bears witness to higher value. If impeded (as when awareness is preoccupied by some other project), the will is cut off from informing action. It does not thereby cease to be the source of value, even when the resulting act is horrific or dehumanizing. Moral error may arise from an insouciance toward duty. But it may also come from an intention to commit evil deeds. In either case, our attitude toward the will rather than the will itself is to blame. No one can will evil for evil's sake alone. Kant says as much when he notes, "The will is absolutely good if it cannot be evil—that is, if its maxim, when made into a universal law, can never be in conflict with itself" (*The Moral Law*, 81).

As to the origin of evil, Kant is unwilling to dismiss blame with respect to a state of forgetfulness. Our habits of escape are formed by inheritance, early influences, and acquired character. Though there is no original evil, these habits are not entirely out of our hands. "Man *himself*," Kant argues, must make or have made himself into whatever, in a moral sense, whether good or evil, he is or is to become. Either condition must be an effect of his will; for otherwise he could not be held responsible for it and could therefore be *morally* neither good nor evil. (*Religion*, 40)

Different aspects of a weak will—lack of steadfastness, impurity of will, or plain wickedness—represent stages of a muting of the moral law. None represents its corruption since it is incorruptible.

Guilt, Redemption, and the Freedom of the Will

Human freedom is exercised in the break from the texture of habit. It resides in "absolute spontaneity." A turn toward awareness of unconditionality or a refusal to do so is equally a manifestation of freedom. We make ourselves into whoever we are from a moral standpoint. The dispositions to vice or virtue that make us up arise from free choice. We are never forced to violate the moral law. Transgression likewise is a consequence of a *chosen* passivity. Our fall into sin comes from a state of innocence.

If our responsibility, in the widest sense, is absolute, so is our guilt. If unconditional awareness is at every moment attainable, then not to attain it places us under an insufferable burden. This conclusion, a difficult one, raises another question. Are we to be forgiven for missing the moral mark? In *The Brothers Karamazov*, Dostoevsky has Ivan argue that absolute freedom (of the kind Kant espouses) implies absolutely no forgiveness. Suppose a man's hunting dogs tear a child to shreds because they were annoyed. The deed is unforgivable on moral ground, even if the victims wish to forgive. Ivan gives three consequences to the intolerable weight of responsibility: sensuality, suicide, or insanity. None is happy; two are precluded by Kant's account of virtue.

Aloysha, Ivan's brother, proposes a fourth possibility: acceptance of the miracle of divine forgiveness. Although not warranted on strict logical grounds, grace is an element of Kant's moral religion. The spirit of gravity (as Nietzsche calls it) may drop from a person's back in a moment of metanoia. Grace allows us to comprehend the horror of our situation—the absolute demand of freedom—but lightly, spryly, with humor. It relieves us of nothing but the oppression of the moral life. The task still remains.

The way to self-knowledge lies in performance of virtue whose special excellence is freedom. Before we become wholly ourselves, immovable obstacles exist. Habits of ego-gratification may remain opaque to efforts of consciousness, no matter how we try. At best, we give a halfhearted willingness. Like Saint Augustine, we may cry, "Lord, save me! But not now!" Kant allows that radical conversion may occur in the throes of despair. A wholehearted embrace of virtue

> cannot be brought about through gradual *reformation* so long as the basis of the maxims remains impure, but must be effected through a *revolution* in the man's disposition (a going over to the maxim of holiness of the disposition). He can become a new man only by a kind of rebirth, as it were a new creation and a change of heart. (*Religion*, 43)

Even an act of grace cannot do our moral work for us. At best, it opens the door, permitting us, if we choose, to enter into redemption. Awakened, we are more receptive to what Kant calls moral sentiments. Nonetheless, we as seekers of truth take final responsibility for the way. As Kant reminds us,

> If a man reverses, by a single unchangeable decision, that highest ground of his maxims whereby he was an evil man (and thus puts on the new man), he is, so far as his principle and cast of mind are concerned, a subject susceptible of goodness, but only in continuous labor and growth is he a good man. (*Religion*, 43)

The Essay
The Critique of Judgement

The first two *Critiques* express but do not exhaust the tremendous power of Kant's philosophical researches. Separately they provide novel approaches in epistemology and ethics while together they explore the border between a personal, relative consciousness and a transpersonal, absolute one. At a later point, Kant produced a third *Critique*, The *Critique of Judgement*. Although it contains some fresh insight, it lacks the integrity and originality of the earlier works. More like a sequel, it weaves together three or four essays whose center lies in the idea of purpose.

Scientific Truth

The introductory essay focuses on purposive explanation in the sciences. Judgement as "a middle term between understanding and reason" describes and formulates the contents of consciousness (reason) insofar as they relate to the objective world (understanding) (*Critique of Judgement*, I, 177). Consistent with the root meaning of the term, judgement exercises a power of decision over the objects of the field. It assays the things

that are present and the relations they enjoy with one
another. Lacking judgement, we would be able neither to
differentiate one thing from the other nor to perceive
their common ground.

Judgement has another, more global function with
respect to scientific knowledge. Kant tells us that "the
principle of judgement, in respect of the form of the
things of nature under empirical laws generally, is the
finality of nature in its multiplicity" (*Critique of
Judgement*, I, 180). Judgement ensures that diverse natural processes of divergent scale—cellular mitosis, conti-
nental drift, and galactic implosion—belong to a single
harmonious whole. To assume the unity of nature per-
mits workers in different scientific fields to have confidence that their results disclose one and the same reality.

That nature is governed by single-minded purpose
is, however, a synthetic *a priori* principle. Constructed by
mind, it is projected onto the plane of sensory experience. Finality in nature is, as Kant distinguished in the
first *Critique*, a regulative, not a constitutive principle.
Regulative principles are

> subjective principles which are derived, not from the
> constitution of an object but from the interest of rea-
> son in respect of a certain possible perfection of the
> knowledge of the object. (*Critique of Pure Reason* B,
> 694)

Other principles of paramount importance enjoy a similar
status, for instance, uniformity of nature, which states
that nature is free from radical, sudden, alogical disjunc-
tions in its daily operation. But we should not be trou-
bled that its objectivity is mind-made. Objectivity in the
sciences requires principles of organization independent
of data. Furthermore, there is growing interest in the idea

that nature conforms to consciousness. The so-called anthropic principle holds that a pre-established harmony between the cosmos and human awareness exists by design, not by accident.

Aesthetic Truth

In the first major division of the *Critique of Judgement*, Kant examines aesthetic experience. "Aesthetic" in the context of the third *Critique* takes on our modern sense—appreciation of artfulness and beauty—and leaves behind the older meaning prevalent in the first *Critique*—that which pertains to the senses. Though his parochial habits deprived him of exposure to great art, Kant had a lifelong interest in natural beauty and its sublimity. The logical and not the experiential basis of aesthetic judgement is the prime focus of his thinking.

Hume argues in the *Treatise on Human Nature* that judgements of taste derive from feeling. They give expression, in logical form, to emotions stirred by an object of art. For Hume, their origin is to be found in the force of sympathy; for instance, the "idea of beauty cannot be accounted for but by sympathy" (*Treatise* II.ii.5). At the same time, aesthetic judgements seem to possess an authority more powerful than that of feeling. They lay claim to a universal validity. On Hume's account, the claim is based on a habitual reaction to a beautiful work of art. The fact that the general population reacts similarly does not negate the subjective and relative authority of the judgement.

In his way, Kant agrees with Hume's assessment but not with his diagnosis of aesthetic experience. One's pleasurable response to beauty is unlike a response to the pleasure of a backrub or an ice-cream cone. Possession or consumption does not enter into the experience. A disinterested delight, contemplative in form, awakens a special sense of appreciation. Disinterestedness itself lends aesthetic judgment the misleading appearance of objectivity. We are misled, Kant argues, because for aesthetic experience, the "determining ground is the feeling of the Subject, and not any concept of an Object" (*Critique of Judgement*, I, 231). Objectivity is non-existent since we lack the requisite concepts of our understanding for aesthetic matters.

The experience of play is important in aesthetic appreciation. In it lies the origin of disinterested delight and apparent universality alike. We are cognitively unencumbered since no concepts apply to this range of our experience while at the same time we are not impelled by a desire for the object. The special combination creates a "state of *free play* of the cognitive faculties attending a representation by which an object is given" and which in turn "must admit of universal communication" (*Critique of Judgement*, I, 217). Kant is even more explicit:

> Since the delight is not based on any inclination of the Subject (or on any other deliberate interest), but the Subject feels himself completely *free* in respect of the liking which he accords to the object, he can find as reason for his delight no personal conditions to which his own subjective self might alone be party. Hence he must regard it as resting on what he may also presuppose in every other person; and therefore he must believe that he has reason for demanding a similar delight from every one. (*Critique of Judgement*, I, 211)

The conclusion is an interesting one. Aesthetic experience mimics the universality of, say, moral experience since ego-consciousness relaxes its grip of control.

Concept and desire no longer determine an outcome. Play is allowed to be free. We are moved by the sense of freedom, yet at the same time, we are not yet related to the unconditional. A foretaste of a greater freedom, this freedom of play is strictly relative. Art serves to remind humanity of a way toward liberation.

Teleology

In the second main section of this *Critique*, Kant examines teleological concepts and judgment *per se*. That he maintains a skeptical attitude toward their validity is consistent with his distrust of ontology. Teleological ideas point to goals, ends, final causes, or destinies. They speak of that for the sake of which a process occurs as the reason for its occurrence. To install them in a conceptual frame is to invite the argument from design as a proof of God's existence.

In a familiar way, Kant maintains that teleology is a regulative, but not a constitutive principle. In a negative way, it helps shape thinking about the objective world. Experiment and experience, however, yield no evidence for or against a teleological principle. The idea

> only signifies a principle of the reflective, and not of the determinant, judgement, and consequently is not meant to introduce any special ground of causality, but only to assist the employment of reason by supplementing investigation on mechanical laws by the addition of another method of investigation. . . .
> (*Critique of Judgement*, II, 383)

Teleological ideas do not determine an event conceptually; rather they simply allow us to make an estimate of an event.

The question of why teleology is anathema to objective thinking reveals a deep layer of supposition. It sheds
light on Kant's fundamental attitudes toward object-consciousness. Wondering why there is no natural science of
final causes, he confesses:

> This is done in order to keep the study of the
> mechanical aspect of nature in close adherence to
> what we are able so to subject to our observation or
> experiment that we could ourselves produce it like
> nature, or at least produce it according to similar
> laws. For we have complete insight only into what
> we can make and accomplish according to our con-
> ceptions. But to effect by means of art a presentation
> similar to organization, as an intrinsic end of nature,
> infinitely surpasses all our powers. (*Critique of
> Judgement*, II, 384)

In the end, science and objectivity are manifestations of
human control. It cannot be relinquished without surren-
dering the proud accomplishments of knowledge of the
natural world. Even though teleology promises an analysis of destiny and final end, it must be sacrificed. Since
finality seems to look deeply into the unknown, the sacrifice is a costly one. With it, a possible way of bridging
the gap between the conditional and the unconditional
realms is lost.

A Kant Chronology

1775   *Von den verschiedenen Racen der Menschen* (Concerning
        the different Races of Mankind)—announcement of lec-
        tures in 1775

1781   *Kritik der reinen Vernunft,* Second Edition 1787 (Critique
        of Pure Reason, tr. by Kemp Smith, 1929; also by Müller,
        1896, and by Meiklejohn, 1871)

1783   *Prolegomena zu einer jeden künftigen Metaphysik* etc.
        (Prolegomena to any Future Metaphysic, tr. by Mahaffy
        and Bernard, 1915, also by Carus, 1902)

1783   *Ueber Schultz's Versuch einer Anleitung zur Sittenlehre für
        alle Menschen ohne Unterschied der Religion* (Concerning
        Schultz's Attempt at an Introduction to Ethics for all Men
        without Distinction of Religion) in *Räsonnirendes
        Bücherverzeichnis,* Königsberg, 1783

1784   *Idee zu einer allgemeinen Geschichte in weltbürgerlicher
        Absicht* (Idea for a Universal History with Cosmopolitan
        Intent, tr. by Friedrich, 1949) in *Berlinische Monatsschrift,*
        Nov. 1784

1784   *Beantwortung der Frage: Was ist Aufklärung?* (What is
        Enlightenment? tr. by Beck, 1949; also by Friedrich, 1949,
        and by Richardson, 1798) in *Berlinische Monatsschrift,*
        Dec. 1784

1785   *Recension von Herders Ideen zur Philosophie der
        Geschichte der Menschheit* (Review of Herder's Ideas con-
        cerning the Philosophy of the History of Mankind) in
        Jenaische Allgemeine Litteratur-Zeitung, 1785

1785   *Grundlegung zur Metaphysik der Sitten* (Groundwork of
        the Metaphysic of Morals, tr. by Paton, 1948; also by Beck,
        1949, and by Abbott, 1889)

1786   Death of Frederick the Great

1786   *Was heisst: Sich im Denken Orientieren?* (What is
        Orientation in Thinking?, tr. by Beck, 1949) in *Berlinische
        Monatsschrift,* Oct. 1786

1788   Wöllner's religious edict

1788   *Ueber den Gebrauch teleogischer Principien in der
        Philosophie* (Concerning the Use of Teleological Principles
        in Philosophy) in Wieland's *Deutscher Mercur,* Jan. 1788

1788   *Kritik der praktischen Vernunft* (Critique of Practical
        Reason, tr. by Beck 1949; also by Abbot, 1889)

1790   *Kritik der Urtheilskraft,* Second Edition, 1793 (Critique of
        Judgement, tr. by Meredith, 1911; also by Bernard, 1892)

1791   *Ueber das Misslingen aller philosophischen Versuche in der Theodicee* (On the Failure of all the Philosophical Essays in the Théodicée, tr. by Richardson, 1798) in *Berlinische Monatsschrift*, Sept. 1791

1793   *Ueber den Gemeinspruch: Das mag in der Theorie richtig sein, taugt aber nicht für die Praxis* (On the Saying: That may be true in Theory but does not hold good in Practice, tr. by Richardson, 1798) in *Berlinische Monatsschrift*, Sept. 1793

1793   RELIGION INNHERHALB DER GRENZEN DER BLOSSEN VERNUNFT (Religion within the Limits of Reason Alone— for translations, see above, pp. cxxxv) Second Edition, 1794

1795   *Zum ewigen Frieden* (Eternal Peace, tr. by Beck and Friedrich, 1949; also by Hastie, 1914)

1796   Discontinued his university lectures

1797   *Metaphysik der Sitten* (Metaphysic of Morals, General Introduction and Introduction to Part II, tr. in part by Abbott, 1889, Part I, tr. by Hastie, 1887, and Part II, tr. by Semple, 1836)

1797   Death of Frederick William II; Wöllner dismissed

1797   *Ueber ein vermeintes Recht, aus Menschenliebe zu lügen* (On a Supposed Right to Lie from Altruistic Motives, tr. by Beck, 1949, also by Abbott, 1889) in *Berlinische Blätter*, Sept. 1797

1798   *Der Streit der Facultäten* (The Conflict of the Faculties)

1798   *Anthropologie in pragmatischer Hinsicht abgefasst*, Second Edition, 1800 (Anthropology, Considered from a Pragmatic Viewpoint)

1800   *Vorrede zu Jachmanns Prufung der Kantischen Religionsphilosophie in Hinsicht auf die ihr beigelegte Aenlichkeit mit dem reinen Mysticismus* (Preface to Jachmann's Examination of the Kantian Philosophy of Religion with regard to its alleged Similarity to pure Mysticism)

1803   *Ueber Pädagogik* (The Educational Theory of Immanuel Kant, tr. by E.F. Buchner, 1904) edited by Rink

1804   Died in Königsberg

1817   *Vorlesungen über die philosophische Religionslehre* (Lectures on the Philosophy of Religion) edited by Pölitz. Second Edition, 1830

1920   *Kants Opus Postumum dargestellt und beurteilt* by Erich
        Adickes
1924   *Eine Vorlesung Kants über Ethik* (Lectures on Ethics, tr. by
        Infield, 1930) edited by Menzer
1936   *Opus Postumum, Erste Hälfte*, edited by Buchenau
1938   *Opus Postumum, Zweite Hälfte*, edited by Lehmann

PART TWO
Selections from Kant's Writings

Critique of Pure Reason

tr. Norman Kemp Smith.
London: Macmillan, 1929

(pp. 7–10)

PREFACE TO FIRST EDITION

Human reason has this peculiar fate that in one species of its knowledge it is burdened by questions which, as prescribed by the very nature of reason itself, it is not able to ignore, but which, as transcending all its powers, it is also not able to answer.

The perplexity into which it thus falls is not due to any fault of its own. It begins with principles which it has no options save to employ in the course of experience, and which this experience at the same time abundantly justifies it in using. Rising with their aid (since it is determined to this also by its own nature) to ever higher, ever more remote, conditions, it soon becomes aware that in this way—the questions never ceasing—its work must always remain incomplete; and it therefore finds itself compelled to resort to principles which overstep all possible empirical employment, and which yet seem so unobjectionable that even ordinary consciousness readily accepts them. But by this procedure human reason precipitates itself into darkness and contradictions; and while it may indeed conjecture that these must be in some way due to concealed errors, it is not in a position to be able to detect them. For since the principles of which it is making use transcend the limits of experience, they are no longer subject to any empirical test. The battle-field of these endless controversies is called metaphysics.

Time was when metaphysics was entitled the Queen of all the sciences; and if the will be taken for the deed, the preeminent importance of her accepted tasks gives her every right to this title of honour. Now, however, the changed fashion of the time brings her only scorn; a matron outcast and forsaken, she mourns like Hecuba: *Modo maxima rerum, tot generis natisque potens—nunc trahor exul, inops.* [Ovid, *Metam.* [xiii. 508–510].]

Her government, under the administration of the *dogmatists*, was at first *despotic*. But inasmuch as the legislation still bore traces of the ancient barbarism, her empire gradually through intestine wars gave way to complete anarchy; and the *sceptics*, a species of nomads, despising all settled modes of life, broke up from time to time all civil society. Happily they were few in number, and were unable to prevent its being established ever anew, although on no uniform and self-consistent plan. In more recent times, it has seemed as if an end might be put to all these controversies and the claims of metaphysics receive final judgment, through a certain *physiology* of the human understanding—that of the celebrated Locke. But it has turned out quite otherwise. For however the attempt be made to cast doubt upon the pretensions of the supposed Queen by tracing her lineage to vulgar origins in common experience, this genealogy has, as a matter of fact, been fictitiously invented, and she has still continued to uphold her claims. Metaphysics has accordingly lapsed back into the ancient time-worn dogmatism, and so again suffers that depreciation from which it was to have been rescued. And now, after all methods, so it is believed, have been tried and found wanting, the prevailing mood is that of weariness and complete *indifferentism*—the mother, in all sciences, of chaos and night, but happily in this case the source, or at least the prelude, of their approaching reform and restoration. For it at least puts an end to that ill-applied industry which has rendered them thus dark, confused, and unserviceable.

But it is idle to feign indifference to such enquiries, the object of which can never be indifferent to our human nature. Indeed these pretended *indifferentists*, however they may try to disguise themselves by substituting a popular tone for the language of the Schools, inevitably fall back, in so far as they think at all, into those very metaphysical assertions which they profess so greatly to despise. None the less this indifference, showing itself in the midst of flourishing sciences, and affecting precisely those sciences, the knowledge of which, if attainable, we should least of all care to dispense with, is a phenomenon that calls for attention and reflection. It is obviously the effect not of levity but of the matured judgment* of the age, which refuses to be any longer put off with illusory knowledge. It is a call to reason to undertake anew the most difficult of all its tasks, namely, that of self-knowledge, and to institute a tribunal which will assure to reason its lawful claims, and dismiss all groundless pretensions, not by despotic decrees, but in accordance with its own eternal and unalterable laws. This tribunal is no other than the *critique of pure reason.*

I do not mean by this a critique of books and systems, but of the faculty of reason in general, in respect of all knowledge after which it may strive *independently of all experience.* It will therefore decide as to the possibility or impossibility of metaphysics in general, and determine its sources, its extent, and its limits—all in accordance with principles.

I have entered upon this path—the only one that has remained unexplored—and flatter myself that in following it I have found a way of guarding against all those errors which have hitherto set reason, in its non-empirical employment, at variance with itself. I have not evaded its questions by pleading the insufficiency of human reason. On the contrary, I have specified these questions exhaustively, according to principles; and after locating the point at which, through misunderstanding, reason comes into conflict with itself, I have solved them to its complete satisfaction. The answer to these questions has not, indeed, been such as a dogmatic and visionary insistence upon knowledge might lead us to expect—that can be catered for only through magical devices, in which I am no adept. Such ways of answering them are, indeed, not within the intention of the natural constitution of our reason; and inasmuch as they have their source in misunderstanding, it is the duty of philosophy to counteract their deceptive influence, no matter what prized and cherished dreams may have to be disowned. In this enquiry I have made completeness my chief aim, and I venture to assert that there is not a single metaphysical problem which has not been solved, or for the solution of which the key at least has not been supplied. Pure reason is, indeed, so perfect a unity that if its principle were insufficient for the solution of even a single one of all of the questions to which it itself gives birth we should have no alternative but to reject the principle, since we should then no longer be able to place implicit reliance upon it in dealing with any one of the other questions.

While I am saying this I can fancy that I detect in the face of the reader an expression of indignation, mingled with contempt, at pretensions seemingly so arrogant and vain-glorious. Yet they are incomparably more moderate than the claims of all those writers who on the lines of the usual programme profess to prove the simple nature of the soul or the necessity of a first beginning of the world. For while such writers pledge themselves to extend human knowledge beyond all limits of possible experience, I humbly confess that this is entirely beyond my power. I have to deal with nothing save reason itself and its pure thinking; and to obtain complete knowledge of these, there is no need to go far afield, since I come upon them in my own self. Common logic itself supplies an example, how all the simple acts of reason can be enumerated completely and systematically. The subject of the present enquiry is the [kindred] question, how much can we hope to achieve by reason, when all the material and assistance of experience are taken away.

---

* We often hear complaints of shallowness of thought in our age and of the consequent decline of sound science. But I do not see that the sciences which rest upon a secure foundation, such as mathematics, physics, etc., in the least deserve this reproach. On the contrary, they merit their old reputation for solidity, and, in the case of physics, even surpass it. The same spirit would have become active in other kinds of knowledge, if only attention had first been directed to the determination of their principles. Till this is done, indifference, doubt, and, in the final issue, severe criticism, are themselves proofs of a profound habit of thought. Our age is, in especial degree, the age of criticism, and to criticism everything must submit. Religion through its sanctity, and law-giving through its majesty, may seek to exempt themselves from it. But they then awaken just suspicion, and cannot claim the sincere respect which reason accords only to that which has been able to sustain the test of free and open examination.

(pp. 45-48)

III. PHILOSOPHY STANDS IN NEED OF A SCIENCE WHICH SHALL DETERMINE THE POSSIBILITY, THE PRINCIPLES, AND THE EXTENT OF ALL *A PRIORI* KNOWLEDGE

But what is still more extraordinary than all the preceding is this, that certain modes of knowledge leave the field of all possible experiences and have the appearance of extending the scope of our judgments beyond all limits of experience, and this by means of concepts to which no corresponding object can ever be given in experience.

It is precisely by means of the latter modes of knowledge, in a realm beyond the world of the senses, where experience can yield neither guidance nor correction, that our reason carries on those enquiries which owing to their importance we consider to be far more excellent, and in their purpose far more lofty, than all that the understanding can learn in the field of appearances. Indeed we prefer to run every risk of error rather than desist from such urgent enquiries, on the ground of their dubious character, or from disdain and indifference. These unavoidable problems set by pure reason itself are *God, freedom, and immortality.* The science which, with all its preparations, is in its final intention directed solely to their solution is metaphysics; and its procedure is at first dogmatic, that is, it confidently sets itself to this task without any previous examination of the capacity or incapacity of reason for so great an undertaking.

Now it does indeed seem natural that, as soon as we have left the ground of experience, we should, through careful enquiries, assure ourselves as to the foundations of any building that we propose to erect, not making use of any knowledge that we possess without first determining whence it has come; and not trusting to principles without knowing their origin. It is natural, that is to say, that the question should first be considered, how the understanding can arrive at all this knowledge *a priori*, and what extent, validity, and worth it may have. Nothing, indeed, could be more natural, if by the term 'natural' we signify what fittingly and reasonably ought to happen. But if we mean by 'natural' what ordinarily happens, then on the contrary nothing is more natural and more intelligible than the fact that this enquiry has been so long neglected. For one part of this knowledge, the mathematical, has long been of established reliability, and so gives rise to a favourable presumption as regards the other part, which may yet be of quite a different nature. Besides, once we are outside the circle of experience, we can be sure of not being *contradicted* by experience. The charm of extending our knowledge is so great that nothing short of encountering a direct contradiction can suffice to arrest us in our course; and this can be avoided, if we are careful in our fabrications—which none the less will still remain fabrications. Mathematics gives us a shining example of how far, independently of experience, we can progress in *a priori* knowledge. It does, indeed, occupy itself with objects and with knowledge solely in so far as they allow of being exhibited in intuition. But this circumstance is easily overlooked, since the intuition, in being thought, can itself be given *a priori*, and is therefore hardly to be distinguished from a bare and pure concept. Misled by such a proof of the power of reason, the demand for the extension of knowledge recognises no limits. The light dove, cleaving the air in her free flight, and feeling its resistance, might imagine that its flight would be still easier in empty space. It was thus that Plato left the world of the senses, as setting too narrow limits to the understanding, and ventured out beyond it on the wings of the ideas, in the empty space of the pure understanding. He did not observe that with all his efforts he made no advance—meeting no resistance that might, as it were, serve as a support upon which he could take a stand, to which he could apply his powers, and so set his understanding in motion. It is, indeed, the common fate of human reason to complete its speculative structures as speedily as may be, and only afterwards to enquire whether the foundations are reliable. All sorts of excuses will then be appealed to, in order to reassure us of their solidity, or rather indeed to enable us to dispense altogether with so late and so dangerous an enquiry. But what keeps us, during the actual building, free from all apprehension and suspicion, and flatters us with a seeming thoroughness, is this other circumstance, namely, that a great, perhaps the greatest, part of the business of our reason consists in analysis of the concepts which we already have of objects. This analysis supplies us with a considerable body of knowledge, which, while nothing but explanation or elucidation of what has already been thought in our concepts, though in a confused manner, is yet prized as being, at least as regards its form, new insight. But so far as the matter or content is concerned, there has been no extension of our previously possessed concepts, but only an analysis of them. Since this procedure yields real knowledge *a priori*, which progresses in an assured and useful fashion, reason is so far misled as surreptitiously to introduce, with out itself being aware of so doing, assertions of an entirely different order, in which it attaches to given concepts others completely foreign to them, and moreover attaches them *a priori*. And yet it is not known how reason can be in position to do this. Such a question is never so much as thought of. I shall therefore at once proceed to deal with the difference between these two kinds of knowledge.

(pp. 82–89)

General Observations on Transcendental Aesthetic

I. To avoid all misapprehension, it is necessary to explain, as clearly as possible, what our view is regarding the fundamental constitution of sensible knowledge in general.

What we have meant to say is that all our intuition is nothing but the representation of appearance; that the things which we intuit are not in themselves what we intuit them as being, nor their relations so constituted in themselves as they appear to us, and that if the subject, or even only the subjective constitution of the senses in general, be removed, the whole constitution and all the relations of objects in space and time, nay space and time themselves, would vanish. As appearances, they cannot exist in themselves, but only in us. What objects may be in themselves, and apart from all this receptivity of our sensibility, remains completely unknown to us. We know nothing but our mode of perceiving them—a mode which is peculiar to us, and not necessarily shared in by every being, though, certainly, by every human being. With this alone have we any concern. Space and time are its pure forms, and sensation in general its matter. The former alone can we know *a priori*, that is, prior to all actual perception; and such knowledge is therefore called pure intuition. The latter is that in our knowledge which leads to its being called *a posteriori* knowledge, that is, empirical intuition. The former inhere in our sensibility with absolute necessity, no matter of what kind our sensations may be; the latter can exist in varying modes. Even if we could bring our intuition to the highest degree of clearness, we should not thereby come any nearer to the constitution of objects in themselves. We should still know only our mode of intuition, that is, our sensibility. We should, indeed, know it completely, but always only under the conditions of space and time—conditions which are originally inherent in the subject. What the objects may be in themselves would never become known to us even through the most enlightened knowledge of that which is alone given to us, namely, their appearance.

The concept of sensibility and of appearance would be falsified, and our whole teaching in regard to them would be rendered empty and useless, if we were to accept the view that our entire sensibility is nothing but a confused representation of things, containing only what belongs to them in themselves, but in doing so under an aggregation of characters and partial representations that we do not consciously distinguish. For the difference between a confused and a clear representation is merely logical, and does not concern the content. No doubt the concept of 'right', in its common-sense usage, contains all that the subtlest speculation can develop out of it, though in its ordinary and practical use we are not conscious of the manifold representations comprised in this thought. But we cannot say that the common concept is therefore sensible, containing a mere appearance. For 'right' can never be an appearance; it is a concept in the understanding, and represents a property (the moral property) of actions, which belongs to them in themselves. The representation of a body in intuition, on the other hand, contains nothing that can belong to an object in itself, but merely the appearance of something, and the mode in which we are affected by that something; and this receptivity of our faculty of knowledge is termed sensibility. Even if that appearance could become completely transparent to us, such knowledge would remain *toto coelo* different from knowledge of the object in itself.

The philosophy of Leibniz and Wolff, in thus treating the difference between the sensible and the intelligible as merely logical, has given a completely wrong direction to all investigations into the nature and origin of our knowledge. This difference is quite evidently transcendental. It does not merely concern their [logical] form, as being either clear or confused. It concerns their origin and content. It is not that by our sensibility we cannot know the nature of things in themselves in any save a confused fashion; we do not apprehend them in any fashion whatsoever. If our subjective constitution be removed, the represented object, with the qualities which sensible intuition bestows upon it, is nowhere to be found, and cannot possibly be found. For it is this subjective constitution which determines its form as appearance.

We commonly distinguish in appearances that which is essentially inherent in their intuition and holds for sense in all human beings, from that which belongs to their intuition accidentally only, and is valid not in relation to sensibility in general but only in relation to a particular standpoint or to a peculiarity of structure in this or that sense. The former kind of knowledge is then declared to represent the object in itself, the latter is its appearance only. But this distinction is merely empirical. If, as generally happens, we stop short at this point, and do not proceed, as we ought, to treat the empirical intuition as itself mere appearance, in which nothing that belongs to a thing in itself can be found, our transcendental distinction is lost. We then believe that we know things in themselves, and this in spite of the fact that in the world of sense, however deeply we enquire into its object, we have to do with nothing but appearances. The rainbow in a sunny shower may be called a mere appearance, and the rain the thing in itself. This is correct, if the latter concept be taken in a merely physical sense. Rain will then be viewed only as that which, in all experience and in all its various positions relative to the senses, is determined thus, and not otherwise, in our intuition. But if we take this empirical object in its general character, and ask, without considering whether or not it is the same for all human sense, whether it represents an object in itself (and by that we cannot mean the drops of rain, for these are already, as appearances, empirical objects), the question as to the relation of the representation to the object at once becomes transcendental. We then realise that not only are the drops of rain mere appearances, but that even their round shape, nay even the space in which they fall, are nothing in themselves, but merely modifications or fundamental forms of our sensible intuition, and that the transcendental object remains unknown to us.

The second important concern of our Transcendental Aesthetic is that it should not obtain favour merely as a plausible hypothesis, but should have that certainty and freedom from doubt which is required of any theory that is to serve as an organon. To make this certainty completely convincing, we shall select a case by which the validity of the position adopted will be rendered obvious, and which will serve to set what has been said in §.3 in a clearer light [not included in present selection; see Norman Kemp Smith translation].

Let us suppose that space and time are in themselves

objective, and are conditions of the possibility of things in themselves. In the first place, it is evident that in regard to both there is a large number of *a priori* apodeictic and synthetic propositions. This is especially true of space, to which our chief attention will therefore be directed in this enquiry. Since the propositions of geometry are synthetic *a priori*, and are known with apodeictic certainty, I raise the question, whence do you obtain such propositions, and upon what does the understanding rely in its endeavour to achieve such absolutely necessary and universally valid truths? There is no other way than through concepts or through intuitions, and these are given either *a priori* or *a posteriori*. In their latter form, namely, as *empirical* concepts, and also as that upon which these are grounded, the *empirical* intuition, neither the concepts nor the intuitions can yield any synthetic proposition except such as is itself also merely empirical (that is, a proposition of experience), and which for that very reason can never possess the necessity and absolute universality which are characteristic of all geometrical propositions. As regards the first and sole means of arriving at such knowledge, namely, in *a priori* fashion through mere concepts or through intuitions, it is evident that from mere concepts only analytic knowledge, not synthetic knowledge, is to be obtained. Take, for instance, the proposition, "Two straight lines cannot enclose a space, and with them alone no figure is possible", and try to derive it from the concept of straight lines and of the number two. Or take the proposition, "Given three straight lines, a figure is possible", and try, in like manner, to derive it from the concepts involved. All your labour is in vain; and you find that you are constrained to have recourse to intuition, as is always done in geometry. You therefore give yourself an object in intuition. But of what kind is this intuition? Is it a pure *a priori* intuition or an empirical intuition? Were it the latter, no universally valid proposition could ever arise out of it—still less an apodeictic proposition—for experience can never yield such. You must therefore give yourself an object *a priori* in intuition, and ground upon this your synthetic proposition. If there did not exist in you a power of *a priori* intuition; and if that subjective condition were not also at the same time, as regards its form, the universal *a priori* condition under which alone the object of this outer intuition is itself possible; if the object (the triangle) were something in itself, apart from any relation to you, the subject, how could you say that what necessarily exist in you as subjective conditions for the construction of a triangle, must of necessity belong to the triangle itself? You could not then add anything new (the figure) to your concepts (of three lines) as something which must necessarily be met with in the object, since this object is [on that view] given antecedently to your knowledge, and not by means of it. If, therefore, space (and the same is true of time) were not merely a form of your intuition, containing conditions *a priori*, under which alone things can be outer objects to you, and without which subjective conditions outer objects are in themselves nothing, you could not in regard to outer objects determine anything whatsoever in an *a priori* and synthetic manner. It is, therefore, not merely possible or probable, but indubitably certain, that space and time, as the necessary conditions of all outer and inner experience, are merely subjective conditions of all our intuition, and that in relation to these conditions all objects are therefore mere appearances, and not given to us as things in themselves which exist in this manner. For this reason also, while much can be said *a priori* as regards the form of appearances, nothing whatsoever can be asserted of the thing in itself, which may underlie these appearances.

II. In confirmation of this theory of the ideality of both outer and inner sense, and therefore of all objects of the senses, as mere appearances, it is especially relevant to observe that everything in our knowledge which belongs to intuition—feeling of pleasure and pain, and the will, not being knowledge, are excluded—contains nothing but mere relations; namely, of locations in a intuition (extension), of change of location (motion), and of laws according to which this change is determined (moving forces). What it is that is present in this or that location, or what it is that is operative in the things themselves apart from change of location, is not given through intuition. Now a thing in itself cannot be known through mere relations; and we may therefore conclude that since outer sense gives us nothing but mere relations, this sense can contain in its representation only the relation of an object to the subject, and not the inner properties of the object in itself. This also holds true of inner sense, not only because the representations of the *outer senses* constitute the proper material with which we occupy our mind, but because the time in which we set these representations, which is itself antecedent to the consciousness of them in experience, and which underlies them as the formal condition of the mode in which we posit them in the mind, itself contains [only] relations of succession, coexistence, and of that which is coexistent with succession, the enduring. Now that which, as representation, can be antecedent to any and every act of thinking anything, is intuition; and if it contains nothing but relations, it is the form of intuition. Since this form does not represent anything save in so far as something is posited in the mind, it can be nothing but the mode in

which the mind is affected through its own activity
(namely, through this positing of its representation), and
so is affected by itself; in other words, it is nothing but
an inner sense in respect of the form of that sense.
Everything that is represented through a sense is so far
always appearance, and consequently we must either
refuse to admit that there is an inner sense, or we must
recognise that the subject, which is the object of the
sense, can be represented through it only as appearance,
not as that subject would judge of itself if its intuition
were self-activity only, that is, were intellectual. The
whole difficulty is as to how a subject can inwardly intuit
itself; and this is a difficulty common to every theory.
The consciousness of self (apperception) is the simple
representation of the 'I', and if all that is manifold in the
subject were given by the *activity of the self*, the inner
intuition would be intellectual. In man this consciousness
demands inner perception of the manifold which is
antecedently given in the subject, and the mode in which
this manifold is given in the mind must, as non-sponta-
neous, be entitled sensibility. If the faculty of coming to
consciousness of oneself is to seek out (to apprehend)
that which lies in the mind, it must affect the mind, and
only in this way can it give rise to an intuition of itself.
But the form of this intuition, which exists antecedently
in the mind, determines, in the representation of time,
the mode in which the manifold is together in the mind,
since it then intuits itself not as it would represent itself if
immediately self-active, but as it is affected by itself, and
therefore as it appears to itself, not as it is.

III. When I say that the intuition of outer objects and
the self-intuition of the mind alike represent the objects
and the mind, in space and in time, as they affect our
senses, that is, as they appear, I do not mean to say that

these objects are a mere *illusion*. For in an appearance the objects, nay even the properties that we ascribe to them, are always regarded as something actually given. Since, however, in the relation of the given object to the subject, such properties depend upon the mode of intuition of the subject, this object as *appearance* is to be distinguished from itself as object in *itself*. Thus when I maintain that the quality of space and of time, in conformity with which, as a condition of their existence, I posit both bodies and my own soul, lies in my mode of intuition and not in those objects in themselves, I am not saying that bodies merely *seem* to be outside me, or that my soul only *seems* to be given in my self-consciousness. It would be my own fault, if out of that which I ought to reckon as appearance, I made mere illusion. That does not follow as a consequence of our principle of the ideality of all our sensible intuitions—quite the contrary. It is only if we ascribe *objective reality* to these forms of representation, that it becomes impossible for us to prevent everything being thereby transformed into mere *illusion*. For if we regard space and time as properties which, if they are to be possible at all, must be found in things in themselves, and if we reflect on the absurdities in which we are then involved, in that two infinite things, which are not substances, nor anything actually inhering in substances, must yet have existence, nay, must be the necessary condition of the existence of all things, and moreover must continue to exist, even although all existing things be removed,—we cannot blame the good Berkeley for degrading bodies to mere illusion. Nay, even our own existence, in being made thus dependent upon the self-subsistent reality of a non-entity, such as time, would necessarily be changed with it into sheer illusion—an absurdity of which no one has yet been guilty.

(pp. 133–138)

3. *The Synthesis of Recognition in a Concept*

If we were not conscious that what we think is the same as what we thought a moment before, all reproduction in the series of representations would be useless. For it would in its present state be a new representation which would not in any way belong to the act whereby it was to be gradually generated. The manifold of the representation would never, therefore, form a whole, since it would lack that unity which only consciousness can impart to it. If, in counting, I forget that the units, which now hover before me, have be en added to one another in succession, I should never know that a total is being produced through this successive addition of unit to unit, and so would remain ignorant of the number. For the concept of the number is nothing but the consciousness of this unity of synthesis.

The word 'concept' might of itself suggest this remark. For this unitary consciousness is what combines the manifold, successively intuited, and thereupon also reproduced, into one representation. This consciousness may often be only faint, so that we do not connect it with the act itself, that is, not in any direct manner with the *generation* of the representation, but only with the outcome [that which is thereby represented]. But notwithstanding these variations, such consciousness, however indistinct, must always be present; without it, concepts, and therewith knowledge of objects, are altogether impossible.

At this point we must make clear to ourselves what we mean by the expression 'an object of representations'. We have stated above that appearances are themselves nothing but sensible representations, which, as such and in themselves, must not be taken as objects capable of existing outside our power of representation. What, then, is to be understood when we speak of an object corresponding to, and consequently also distinct from, our knowledge? It is easily seen that this object must be thought only as something in general = x, since outside our knowledge we have nothing which we could set over against this knowledge as corresponding to it.

Now we find that our thought of the relation of all knowledge to its object carries with it an element of necessity; the object is viewed as that which prevents our modes of knowledge from being haphazard or arbitrary, and which determines them *a priori* in some definite fashion. For in so far as they are to relate to an object, they must necessarily agree with one another, that is, must possess that unity which constitutes the concept of an object.

But it is clear that, since we have to deal only with the manifold of our representations, and since that x (the object) which corresponds to them is nothing to us— being, as it is, something that has to be distinct from all our representations—the unity which the object makes necessary can be nothing else than the formal unity of consciousness in the synthesis of the manifold of representations. It is only when we have thus produced synthetic unity in the manifold of intuition that we are in a position to say that we know the object. But this unity is impossible if the intuition cannot be generated in accordance with a rule by means of which a function of synthesis as makes the reproduction of the manifold *a priori* necessary, and renders possible a concept in which it is united. Thus we think a triangle as an object, in that we are conscious of the combination of three straight lines according to a rule by which such an intuition can always be represented. This *unity of rule* determines all the manifold, and limits it to conditions which make the unity of apperception possible. The concept of this unity is the representation of the object = x, which I think through the predicates, above mentioned, of a triangle.

All knowledge demands a concept, though that concept may, indeed, be quite imperfect or obscure. But a concept is always, as regards its form, something universal which serves as a rule. The concept of body, for instance, as the unity of the manifold which is thought through it, serves as a rule in our knowledge of outer appearances. But it can be a rule for intuitions only in so far as it rep resents in any given appearances the necessary reproduction of their manifold, and thereby the synthetic unity in our consciousness of them. The concept of body, in the perception of something outside us, necessitates the representation of extension, and therewith representations of impenetrability, shape, etc.

All necessity, without exception, is grounded in a transcendental condition. There must, therefore, be a transcendental ground of the unity of consciousness in the synthesis of the manifold of all our intuitions, and consequently also of the concepts of objects in general, and so of all the objects of experience, a ground without which it would be impossible to think any object for our intuitions; for this object is no more than that something, the concept of which expresses such a necessity of synthesis.

This original and transcendental condition is no other than *transcendental apperception*. Consciousness of self according to the determination of our state in inner perception is always empirical, and always changing. No fixed and abiding self can present itself in this flux of inner appearances. Such consciousness is usually named *inner sense*, or *empirical apperception*. What has *necessarily* to be represented as numerically identical cannot be thought of as such through empirical data. To render such a transcendental presupposition valid, there must be a condition which precludes all experience, and which makes experience itself possible.

There can be in us no modes of knowledge, no connection or unity of one mode of knowledge with another, without that unity of consciousness which precedes all data of intuitions, and by relation to which representation of objects is alone possible. This pure original unchangeable consciousness I shall name *transcendental apperception*. That it deserves this name is clear from the fact that even the purest objective unity, namely, that of the *a priori* concepts (space and time), is only possible through relation of the intuitions to such unity of consciousness. The numerical unity of this apperception is thus the *a priori* ground of all concepts, just as the manifoldness of space and time is the *a priori* ground of the intuitions of sensibility.

This transcendental unity of apperception forms out of all possible appearances, which can stand alongside one another in one experience, a connection of all these representations according to laws. For this unity of consciousness would be impossible if the mind in knowledge of the manifold could not become conscious of the identity of function whereby it synthetically combines it in one knowledge. The original and necessary consciousness of the identity of the self is thus at the same time a consciousness of an equally necessary unity of the synthesis of all appearances according to concepts, that is, according to rules, which not only make them necessarily reproducible but also in so doing determine an object for their intuition, that is, the concept of something wherein they are necessarily interconnected. For the mind could never think its identity in the manifoldness of its representations, and indeed think this identity *a priori*, if it did not have before its eyes the identity of its act, whereby it subordinates all synthesis of apprehension (which is empirical) to a transcendental unity, thereby rendering possible their interconnection according to *a priori* rules.

Now, also, we are in a position to determine more adequately our concept of an *object* in general. All representations have, as representations, their object, and can themselves in turn become objects of other representations. Appearances are the sole objects which can be given to us immediately, and that in them which relates immediately to the object is called intuition. But these appearances are not things in themselves; they are only representations, which in turn have their object—an object which cannot itself be intuited by us, and which may, therefore, be named the non-empirical, that is, transcendental object = *x*.

The pure concept of this transcendental object, which in reality throughout all our knowledge is always one and the same, is what can alone confer upon all our empirical concepts in general relation to an object, that is, objective reality. This concept cannot contain any determinate intuition, and therefore refers only to that unity which must be met with in any manifold of knowledge which stands in relation to an object. This relation is nothing but the necessary unity of consciousness, and therefore also of the synthesis of the manifold, through a common function of the mind, which combines it in one representation. Since this unity must be regarded as necessary *a priori*—otherwise knowledge would be without an object—the relation to a transcendental object, that is, the objective reality of our empirical knowledge, rests on the transcendental law, that all appearances, in so far as through them objects are to be given to us, must stand under those *a priori* rules of synthetical unity whereby the interrelating of these appearances in empirical intuition is alone possible. In other words, appearances in experience must stand under the conditions of the necessary unity of apperception, just as in mere intuition they must be subject to the formal conditions of space and of time. Only thus can any knowledge become possible at all.

(pp. 264–270)

Thought is the act which relates given intuition to an object. If the mode of this intuition is not in any way given, the object is merely transcendental, and the concept of understanding has only transcendental employment, namely, as the unity of the thought of a manifold in general. Thus no object is determined through a pure category in which abstraction is made of every condition of sensible intuition—the only kind of intuition possible to us. It then expresses only the thought of an object in general, according to different modes. Now the employment of a concept involves a function of judgement whereby an object is subsumed under the concept, and so involves at least the formal condition under which something can be given in intuition. If this condition of judgment (the schema) is lacking, all subsumption becomes impossible. For in that case nothing is given that could be subsumed under the concept. The merely transcendental employment of the categories is, therefore, really no employment at all, and has no determinate object, not even one that is determinable in its mere form. It therefore follows that the pure category does not suffice for a synthetic *a priori* principle, that the principles of pure understanding are only of empirical, never of transcendental employment, and that outside the field of possible experience there can be no synthetic *a priori* principles.

It may be advisable, therefore, to express the situation as follows. The pure categories, apart from formal conditions of sensibility, have only transcendental meaning; nevertheless they may not be employed transcendentally, such employment being in itself impossible, inasmuch as all conditions of any employment in judgments are lacking to them, namely, the formal conditions of the subsumption of any ostensible object under these concepts. Since, then, as pure categories merely, they are not to be employed empirically, and cannot be employed transcendentally, they cannot, when separated from all sensibility, be employed in any manner whatsoever, that is, they cannot be applied to any ostensible object. They are the pure form of the employment of understanding in respect of objects in general, that is, of thought; but since they are merely its form, through them alone no object can be thought or determined.

But we are here subject to an illusion from which it is difficult to escape. The categories are not, as regards their origin, grounded in sensibility, like the *forms of intuition*, space and time; and they seem, therefore, to allow of an application extending beyond all object of the senses. As a matter of fact they are nothing but *forms of thought*, which contain the merely logical faculty of uniting *a priori* in one consciousness the manifold given in intuition; and apart, therefore, from the only intuition that is possible to us, they have even less meaning than the pure sensible forms. Through these forms an object is at least given, whereas a mode of combining the manifold—a mode peculiar to our understanding—by itself, in the absence of that intuition wherein the manifold can be given, signifies nothing at all. At the same time, if we entitle certain objects, as appearances, sensible entities (phenomena), then since we thus distinguish the mode in which we intuit them from the nature that belongs to them in themselves, it is implied in this distinction that we place the latter, considered in their own nature, although we do not so intuit them, or that we place other possible things, which are not objects of our senses but are thought as objects merely through the understanding, in opposition to the former, and that in so doing we entitle them intelligible entities (noumena). The question then arises, whether our pure concepts of understanding have meaning in respect of these latter, and so can be a way of knowing them.

At the very outset, however, we come upon an ambiguity which may occasion serious misapprehension. The understanding, when its entitles an object in a [certain] relation mere phenomenon, at the same time forms, apart from that relation, a representation of an *object in itself*, and so comes to represent itself as also being able to form *concepts* of such objects. And since the understanding yields concepts additional to the categories, it also supposes that the object in itself must at least be *thought* through these pure concepts, and so is misled into treating the entirely *indeterminate* concept of an intelligible entity, namely, of a something in general outside our sensibility, as being a *determinate* concept of an entity that allows of being known in a certain [purely intelligible] manner by means of the understanding.

If by 'noumenon' we mean a thing so far as it is *not an object of our sensible intuition*, and so abstract from our mode of intuiting it, this is a noumenon in the *negative* sense of the term. But if we understand by it an *object* of a *non-sensible intuition*, we thereby presuppose a special mode of intuition, namely, the intellectual, which is not that which we possess, and of which we cannot comprehend even the possibility. This would be 'noumenon' in the *positive* sense of the term.

The doctrine of sensibility is likewise the doctrine of the noumenon in the negative sense, that is, of things which the understanding must think without this reference to our mode of intuition, therefore not merely as appearances but as things in themselves. At the same time the understanding is well aware that in viewing things in this manner, as thus apart from our mode of intuition, it can not make any use of the categories. For the categories have meaning only in relation to the unity of intuition in space and time; and even this unity they can determine, by means of general *a priori* connecting concepts, only because of the mere ideality of space and time. In cases where this unity of time is not to be found, and therefore in the case of noumenon, all employment and indeed the whole meaning of the categories, entirely vanishes; for we have then no means of determining whether things in harmony with the categories are even possible. On this point I need only refer the reader to what I have said in the opening sentences of the *General Note* appended to the preceding chapter [not included in present selection; see Norman Kemp Smith translation]. The possibility of a thing can never be proved merely from the fact that its concept is not self-contradictory, but only though its being supported by some corresponding intuition. If, therefore, we should attempt to apply the categories to objects which are not viewed as being appearances, we should have to postulate an intuition other than the sensible, and the object would thus be a noumenon in the *positive sense*. Since, however, such a type of intuition, intellectual intuition, forms no part whatsoever of our faculty of knowledge, it follows that the employment of the categories can never extend further than to the objects of experience. Doubtless, indeed, there are intelligible objects corresponding to the sensible entities; there may also be intelligible entities to which our sensible faculty of intuition has no relation whatsoever; but our concepts of understanding, being mere forms of thought for our sensible intuition, could not in the least apply to them. That, therefore, which we entitle 'noumenon' must be understood as being such only in a *negative* sense.

Prolegomena to any Future Metaphysics

tr. Peter G. Lucas. Manchester: Manchester University Press, 1953

(pp. 30–35)

GENERAL QUESTION
HOW IS KNOWLEDGE OUT OF PURE REASON POSSIBLE?

§.5

We have seen above the vast difference between analytic and synthetic judgements. The possibility of analytic propositions could be conceived very easily; for it is grounded solely on the principle of contradiction. The possibility of synthetic propositions *a posteriori*, i.e. of propositions that are drawn from experience, also needs no special explanation; for experience itself is nothing other than a continual joining together (synthesis) of perceptions. Thus we are only left with synthetic propositions *a priori*, the possibility of which must be looked for or enquired into, because it must rest on principles other than the principle of contradiction.

But here we cannot rightly start by looking for the

possibility of such propositions, i.e. by asking whether they are possible. For there are plenty of them, really given with undisputed certainty, and as the method which we are now following is to be analytic, we shall start from this: that such synthetic but pure knowledge by reason is real. But then we still have to *enquire* into the ground of this possibility, and ask *how* this knowledge is possible, so as to put ourselves in a position to determine, from the principles of its possibility, the conditions of its employment and the extent and boundaries of the same. Expressed with scholastic precision, the proper problem, on which everything depends, is therefore:

How are synthetic propositions a priori possible?

I have expressed this problem above rather differently, for the sake of popularity, namely as a question about knowledge out of pure reason, which I could well do on this occasion without prejudicing the desired insight, because, as we have to do here solely with metaphysics and its sources, the reader will, I hope, after the foregoing remarks, always remember: that when we speak here of knowledge out of pure reason, it is never a question of analytic but solely of synthetic knowledge.*

Whether metaphysics is to stand or fall, and thus its existence, now entirely depends on the solving of this problem. A man may propound his assertions in metaphysics as plausibly as he will, heaping conclusions on conclusions to suffocation; if he has not first been able to answer this question satisfactorily, I have the right to say: this is all vain groundless philosophy and false wisdom. You speak through pure reason, and presume as it were to create cognitions *a priori*, not merely by analysing given concepts but by giving out that you are making new connections, which do not rest on the principle of contradiction, and you imagine you have insight into them independently of all experience; how do you arrive at all this and how will you justify such pretensions? You cannot be permitted to appeal to the consent of common sense, for this is a witness whose reputation only rests on public rumour.

> Quodcunque ostendis mihi sic, incredulus odi. *Horat.* [Horace: *Epist.* II.3.188. "Whatever you show me thus, I hate and do not believe."]

Indispensable as it is to answer this question, it is equally difficult to do so, and although the principle reason why an answer was not attempted long ago is that it never even occurred to anyone that such a question could be asked, a second reason is that a satisfactory answer to this one question demands much deeper, more persistent and painstaking reflection than the most prolix metaphysical work that ever promised immortality to its author on its first appearance. Every discerning reader who carefully thinks over what this problem demands will be frightened at first by its difficulty, and will hold it to be insoluble, and if it were not that there really are such synthetic cognitions *a priori*, hold it to be wholly impossible. This is what really happened to David Hume, although he did not represent the question to himself in anything like such universality as has been done here and must be done, if the answer is to be decisive for the whole of metaphysics. For how is it possible, said the sagacious man, that if a concept is given to me, I can go beyond it and connect with it another concept that is not contained in it, and connect it as if it belonged *necessarily* to the first concept? Only experience can provide us with such connections (so he argued from this difficulty, taking it for an impossibility), and all this sup-posed necessity, or, what is the same, this supposed knowledge *a priori*, is nothing but a long-standing habit of finding something to be true, and hence of taking sub-jective necessity to be objective.

If the reader complains about the toil and trouble that I am going to give him in solving this problem, he only has to make the attempt to solve it in an easier way himself. Perhaps he will then feel himself obliged to the man who has taken over for him a task of such deep research, and will rather show some surprise that, con-sidering the nature of the matter, it has still been possible to make the solution as easy as it is. It has cost the labour of many years to solve this problem in its full uni-versality (in the sense in which mathematicians take this word, namely covering all cases), and finally also to be able to present it as the reader will find here, in analytic form.

All metaphysicians are therefore solemnly and legal-ly suspended from their business until they have satisfac-torily answered the question: *How are synthetic cognitions a priori possible?* For in this answer alone are to be found the credentials which they must show if they have anything to offer us in the name of pure reason; without these they can only expect to be turned away by all reasonable men, who have so often been deceived, without any further enquiry into what they are offering.

If on the other hand they want to carry on their business not as *science* but as an *art* of wholesome per-suasions suitable for ordinary common sense, they can-not in fairness be prevented from following this trade. They will then speak the modest language of rational belief, they will admit that they are not even allowed to *guess*, let alone to *know*, anything about what lies beyond the bounds of all possible experience, but only to *assume* something (not for speculative use, for they must renounce this, but solely for practical use) that is possible and even indispensable in life for the guidance of the understanding and the will. Only thus will they deserve the name of useful and wise men, the more so, the more they renounce the name of metaphysicians; for metaphysicians aim to be speculative philosophers and since stale probabilities cannot be the target when it is a question of judgements *a priori* (for what is said to be known *a priori* is thereby announced as necessary), they cannot be permitted to play with guesses. What they assert must be science, otherwise it is nothing at all.

It can be said that the whole transcendental philosophy which necessarily precedes all metaphysics is itself nothing other than merely the complete solution of the question proposed here, only in systematic order and in full detail, and that until now we have had no transcendental philosophy; for what bears its name is properly a part of metaphysics; but the former science has first to settle the possibility of the latter, and must therefore precede all metaphysics. Merely to answer one single question adequately, we need a whole science, a science deprived of all assistance from others and in itself wholly new; it is not therefore to be wondered at if the solution to this question is joined with trouble and difficulty and even with some obscurity.

In now proceeding to this solution, according to the analytic method, in which we presuppose that such cognitions out of pure reason are real, we can appeal to only two *sciences* of theoretical knowledge (with which alone we are here concerned), namely *pure mathematics* and *pure natural science*, for only these can represent objects to us in intuition, and if a cognition *a priori* should occur in them, show us *in concreto* its truth, or its agreement with the object, i.e. show us its *reality*, from which we could then go on in the analytic way to the ground of its possibility. This makes things much easier, in that universal considerations, as well as being applied to facts, also start from them, instead of, as in the synthetic procedure, having to be deduced wholly *in abstracto* out of concepts.

In order to ascend from these kinds of pure knowledge *a priori*, which are both real and grounded, to a possible kind of knowledge which we are seeking, namely to metaphysics as science, we must include under our main question that which gives rise to metaphysics—that *a priori* knowledge merely naturally given, though not above suspicion with regard to its truth, which forms the ground of that science, that knowledge, the elaboration of which without any critical enquiry into its possibility is usually called metaphysics, in a word the natural disposition to such a science. The main transcendental question will therefore be divided into four other questions and answered in stages.

1) *How is pure mathematics possible?*
2) *How is pure natural science possible?*
3) *How is metaphysics possible in general?*
4) *How is metaphysics possible as a science?*

It can be seen that although the solution of these problems is mainly designed to exhibit the essential content of the *Critique*, it also has something peculiar to itself which is worth attention for its own sake, namely that we are looking for the sources of given sciences in reason itself, and in so doing investigating and measuring out for reason, by means of the deed itself, its power of knowing anything *a priori*. These sciences themselves then profit by this, if not in respect of their content, yet as concerns their correct employment, and in throwing light on a higher question about their common origin give occasion at the same time for their own nature to be more clearly revealed.

---

* In consequence of the gradual advance of knowledge it is inevitable that certain expressions that have become classical and have been in use since the childhood of science, will be found inadequate and inappropriate, and that a certain new and more suitable usage will run into some danger of being confused with the old. Analytic method, in so far as it opposed to the synthetic method, is something quite different from an aggregate of analytic propositions. It means that one starts from what is being looked for as if it were given, and ascends to the conditions under which alone it is possible. In this method one often uses nothing but synthetic propositions, as in the example of mathematical analysis, and it might be better to call it the *regressive* method, in distinction form the synthetic or *progressive* method. The name analytic also occurs as a principal part of logic, and there it is the logic of truth and is opposed to dialectic, without considering specifically whether the cognitions that belong to it are analytic or synthetic.

(pp. 90–95)

MAIN TRANSCENDENTAL QUESTION
Third Part
HOW IS METAPHYSICS POSSIBLE IN GENERAL?
§.40

A deduction such as we have now made both of pure mathematics and of pure natural science was not needed by either of them *for the sake of their own security* and certainty; for the first is supported on its own evidence; and the second springs from pure sources of reason, although it is supported on experience and thor-

oughgoing confirmation by it, which latter witness it cannot altogether refuse and dispense with because with all
its certainty, it can never, as philosophy, stand equal with
mathematics. Both sciences therefore needed the said
enquiry not for themselves but for another science,
namely metaphysics.

Metaphysics has to do, not merely with concepts of
nature which always find their application in experience,
but also with pure concepts of reason which are never
given in any possible experience whatever, that is, with
concepts whose objective reality (that they are not mere
chimeras) and assertions whose truth or falsehood can
never be confirmed or discovered by any experience.
This part of metaphysics is moreover the one which constitutes the essential end of metaphysics, towards which
everything else is only a means, and thus this science
needs such a deduction *for its own sake*. The third question now before us concerns as it were the kernel of
metaphysics and what is peculiar to it, namely the occu-
pation of reason merely with itself and the acquaintance
with objects which, brooding over its own concepts, it
supposes to arise immediately out of them without need-
ing the mediation of experience or in any way being able
to reach them through experience.*1

Without a solution to this question reason will never
satisfy itself. Use in experience, to which reason limits
pure understanding, will not fulfil reason's own complete
destiny. Every particular experience is only a part of the
whole sphere of the territory of experience; but the
absolute whole of all possible experience is not itself experience and yet is a necessary problem for reason. For the
mere representation of this problem needs concepts quite
different from these pure concepts of the understanding,
the use of which is only *immanent*, i.e. bears on experi-

ence in so far as it can be given. Concepts of reason on the other hand bear on the completeness i.e. the collective unity of all possible experience, thereby going beyond every given experience and becoming *transcendent*.

As the understanding needed categories for experience, so reason contains in itself the ground of ideas, by which I mean necessary concepts, the object of which *can* none the less *not* be given in any experience. Ideas lie in the nature of reason, as categories in the nature of the understanding, and if ideas carry with them an illusion which can easily mislead, this illusion is unavoidable, although "that it shall not seduce into error" can very well be prevented.

As all illusion consists in taking the subjective ground of judgement to be objective, self-knowledge of pure reason in its transcendent (hyperbolical) use will be the only safeguard against the aberrations into which reason falls when it mistakes its destiny, and refers transcendently to the object in itself that only concerns reason's own subject and the conduct of it in all its immanent uses.

---

*1 If it can be said that a science, at least in the idea of all men, is *real* as soon as it has been established that the problems which lead to it are put before everyone by the nature of human reason, and hence at all times many though faulty essays in it are un avoidable, it will also have to be said that metaphysics is subjectively (indeed necessarily) real; and then we can legitimately ask how it is (objectively) possible.

§.41

The distinction of *Ideas*, i.e. of pure concepts of reason, from the categories or pure concepts of the understanding, as knowledge of a quite different kind, origin and use, is so important an item in the grounding of a science which is to contain the system of all this knowledge *a priori*, that without such a separation metaphysics is absolutely impossible or at best an irregular, bungling attempt to build a house of cards without knowledge of the materials with which one is working and of their fitness for one purpose or another. If critique o.p.r. had achieved nothing else than to make this distinction plain for the first time, it would have contributed more to the enlightenment of our comprehension and to the conduct of enquiry in the field of metaphysics than all the fruitless efforts to do justice to the transcendent problems of p.r. that have ever been undertaken; for it was never even suspected that this was quite another field from that of the understanding, and hence that concepts of the understanding and of reason were being mentioned in the same breath, as if they were of the same kind.

§.42

All pure knowledge by the understanding has this in common, that its concepts can be given in experience and its principles confirmed by experience; whereas transcendent knowledge by reason can neither be given, as far as its *ideas* are concerned, in experience, nor its *propositions* ever be confirmed or refuted by experience. Hence the error that may creep in can never be discovered by anything other than pure reason itself, which is very difficult, because this very reason naturally becomes dialectical by means of its ideas, and the illusion which inevitably follows can be held in limits by no objective and dogmatic enquiries into things but merely by subjective enquiries into reason itself as a source of ideas.

§.43

It was always my highest aim in the Critique to see

how I might be able not only carefully to distinguish the kinds of knowledge, but also to deduce all the concepts belonging to each of them from their common source, so that I should not only be able securely to determine their use, being informed about where they were derived from, but also might enjoy the inestimable advantage, never previously anticipated, of knowing completeness in the enumerating, classifying and specifying of the concepts *a priori*, and of knowing it according to principles. Without this everything in metaphysics is nothing but rhapsody, in which one never knows whether one has enough of what one possesses, or whether, and where, something may still be missing. Admittedly this advantage can only be had in pure philosophy, but of this it constitutes the essence.

As I had found the origin of the categories in the four logical functions of all judgements of the understanding, it was quite natural to look for the origin of the ideas in the three functions of syllogisms; because if such pure concepts of reason (transcendental ideas) are once given, they might well be encountered, unless they were held to be innate, nowhere else than in the same act of reason which, in so far as it merely concerns the form, constitutes what is logical in syllogisms, but in so far as it represents the judgements of the understanding as determined in respect of one or the other form *a priori*, constitutes the transcendental concepts of pure reason.

The formal difference of syllogisms makes their division into categorical, hypothetical, and disjunctive necessary. The concepts of reason grounded thereon thus contain first the idea of the complete subject (the substantial), secondly the idea of the complete series of conditions, and thirdly the determination of all concepts in the idea of a complete totality of the possible.*2 The first idea was psychological, the second cosmological, the third theological, and as all three give occasion for a dialectic, but each in its own way, they were the ground for the division of the whole dialectic of pure reason: into the paralogism, the antinomy, and finally the ideal of pure reason, through which deduction we are completely assured that all claims of pure reason are here quite completely represented and not a single one can be missing, because the faculty of reason itself from which alone they take their origin is exhaustively surveyed by it.

---

*2 In the disjunctive judgement we regard *all possibility* as divided in respect of a certain concept. The ontological principle of the thoroughgoing determination of a thing in general (of all possible opposite predicates one is attributable to each thing), which is at the same time the principle of all disjunctive judgements, has as its ground the totality of all possibility, in which the possibility of every thing in general is regarded as determinable. This serves as a little illustration of the above proposition: that the act of reason in disjunctive syllogisms is the same, as to its form, as that through which it brings into being the idea of a totality of all reality, which contains in itself the positive member of all opposite predicates.

§.44

It is further worthy in general of note, while making these considerations: that the ideas of reason are not, like the categories, of any use to us for the employment of the understanding in respect of experience but are entirely dispensable in respect of it, indeed opposed and a hindrance to the maxims of knowledge of nature by reason, although they are necessary to another end that is yet to be determined. Whether the soul is a simple substance or not, is quite indifferent to us for explaining the appearances of the soul; for we cannot make the concept of a simple being understandable sensibly and in concreto by any possible experience, and thus it is quite empty in

respect of all the desired insight into the cause of appearances, and cannot serve as a principle for explaining
what inner or outer experience offers. Nor can we use
the cosmological ideas of the beginning of the world or
of the eternity of the world (*a parte ante*) in order to
explain any event in the world itself. Finally, according to
a correct maxim of natural philosophy, we must refrain
from all explanation of the ordinance of nature drawn
from the will of a highest being, because this is no longer
natural philosophy but an admission that we are coming
to the end of it. These ideas thus have a quite different
determination of their use than the categories, through
which and through the principles built on them experience itself first became possible. Yet our laborious analytic of the understanding would also be quite superfluous
if our aim was directed to nothing other than mere
knowledge of nature as it can be given in experience; for
reason does its job quite safely and well both in mathematics and in natural science without all this subtle
deduction. Thus our critique of the understanding is
linked with the ideas of pure reason to an end which lies
beyond the use of the understanding in experience, and
we have said above that the use of the understanding in
this regard is wholly impossible and without object or
meaning. But there must still be agreement between
what belongs to the nature of reason and of the understanding, and the former must contribute to the perfection of the latter, and cannot possibly confuse it.

The solution of this question is as follows. Pure reason does not, with its ideas, have as its aim particular
objects lying beyond the field of experience, but only
demands completeness in the use of the understanding
in the complex of experience. This completeness can
however only be a completeness of principles, not of

intuitions and objects. None the less, in order to represent this completeness to itself determinately and to bring knowledge by the understanding as near as possible to the completeness which this idea denotes, it thinks of it as knowledge of an object, knowledge of which is completely determined in respect of the rules of the understanding, which object is however only an idea.

The Moral Law

tr. H.J. Paton. London:
Hutchinson University Library,
1948

(pp. 84–109)

[*How are imperatives possible?*]

The question now arises 'How are all these imperatives possible?' This question does not ask how we can
conceive the execution of an action commanded by the
imperative, but merely how we can conceive the necessitation of the will expressed by the imperative in setting
us a task. How an imperative of skill is possible requires
no special discussion. Who wills the end, wills (so far as
reason has decisive influence on his actions) also the
means which are indispensably necessary and in his
power. So far as willing is concerned, this proposition is
analytic: for in my willing of an object as an effect there
is already conceived the causality of myself as an acting
cause—that is, the use of means; and from the concept of
willing an end the imperative merely extracts the concept
of actions necessary to this end. (Synthetic propositions
are required in order to determine the means to a proposed end, but these are concerned, not with the reason
for performing the act of will, but with the cause which
produces the object.) That in order to divide a line into

two equal parts on a sure principle I must from its ends describe two intersecting arcs—this is admittedly taught by mathematics only in synthetic propositions; but when I know that the aforesaid effect can be produced only by such an action, the proposition 'If I fully will the effect, I also will the action required for it' is analytic; for it is the one and the same thing to conceive something as an effect possible in a certain way through me and to conceive myself as acting in the same way with respect to it.

If it were only as easy to find a determinate concept of happiness, the imperatives of prudence would agree entirely with those of skill and would be equally analytic. For here as there it could alike be said 'Who wills the end, wills also (necessarily, if he accords with reason) the sole means which are in his power'. Unfortunately, however, the concept of happiness is so indeterminate a concept that although every man wants to attain happiness, he can never say definitely and in unison with himself what it really is that he wants and wills. The reason for this is that all the elements which belong to the concept of happiness are without exception empirical—that is, they must be borrowed from experience; but that none the less there is required for the Idea of happiness an absolute whole, a maximum of well-being in my present, and in every future, state. Now it is impossible for the most intelligent, and at the same time most powerful, but nevertheless finite, being to form here a determinate concept of what he really wills. Is it riches that he wants? How much anxiety, envy, and pestering might he not bring in this way on his own head! Is it knowledge and insight? This might perhaps merely give him an eye so sharp that it would make evils at present hidden from him and yet unavoidable seem all the more frightful, or would add a load of still further needs to the desires which already give him trouble enough. Is it long life? Who will guarantee that it would not be a long misery? Is it at least health? How often has infirmity of body kept a man from excesses into which perfect health would have let him fall!—and so on. In short, he has no principle by which he is able to decide with complete certainty what will make him truly happy, since for this he would require omniscience. Thus we cannot act on determinate principles in order to be happy, but only on empirical counsels, for example, of diet, frugality, politeness, reserve, and so on—things which experience shows contribute most to well-being on the average. From this it follows that imperatives of prudence, speaking strictly, do not command at all—that is, cannot exhibit actions objectively as practically *necessary*; that they are rather to be taken as recommendations (*consilia*), rather than commands (*praecepta*), of reason; that the problem of determining certainly and universally what action will promote the happiness of a rational being is completely insoluble; and consequently that in regard to this there is no imperative possible which in the strictest sense could command us to do what will make us happy, since happiness is an Ideal, not of reason, but of imagination—an Ideal resting merely on empirical grounds, of which it is vain to expect that they should determine an action by which we could attain the totality of a series of consequences which is in fact infinite. Nevertheless, if we assume that the means to happiness could be discovered with certainty, this imperative of prudence would be an analytic practical proposition; for it differs from the imperative of skill only in this—that in the latter the end is merely possible, while in the former the end is given. In spite of this difference, since both command solely the means to something assumed to be willed as an end, the imperative which commands him who wills the end to will the means is in both cases analytic. Thus there is likewise no difficulty in regard to the possibility of an imperative of prudence.

Beyond all doubt, the question 'How is the imperative of *morality* possible?' is the only one in need of a solution; for it is in no way hypothetical, and consequently we cannot base the objective necessity which it affirms on any presupposition, as we can with hypothetical imperatives. Only we must never forget here that it is impossible to settle *by an example*, and so empirically, whether there is any imperative of this kind at all: we must rather suspect that all imperatives which seem to be categorical may none the less be covertly hypothetical. Take, for example, the saying 'Thou shalt make no false promises'. Let us assume that the necessity for this abstention is no mere advice for the avoidance of some further evil—as it might be said 'You ought not to make a lying promise lest, when this comes to light, you destroy your credit'. Let us hold, on the contrary, that an action of this kind must be considered as bad in itself, and that the imperative of prohibition is therefore categorical. Even so, we cannot with any certainty show by an example that the will is determined here solely by the law without any further motive, although it may appear to be so; for it is always possible that the fear of disgrace, perhaps also hidden dread of other risks, may unconsciously influence the will. Who can prove by experience that a cause is not present? Experience shows only that it is not perceived. In such a case, however, the so-called moral imperative, which as such appears to be categorical and unconditioned, would in fact be only a pragmatic prescription calling attention to our advantage and merely bidding us take this into account.

We shall thus have to investigate the possibility of a *categorical* imperative entirely *a priori*, since here we do not enjoy the advantage of having its reality given in experience and so of being obliged merely to explain, and not to establish, its possibility. So much, however, can be seen provisionally—that the categorical imperative alone purports to be a practical *law*, while all the rest may be called *principles* of the will but not laws; for an action necessary merely in order to achieve an arbitrary purpose can be considered as in itself contingent, and we can always escape from the precept if we abandon the purpose; whereas an unconditioned command does not leave it open to the will to do the opposite at its discretion and therefore alone carries with it that necessity which we demand from a law.

In the second place, with this categorical imperative or law of morality the reason for our difficulty (in comprehending its possibility) is a very serious one. We have here a synthetic *a priori* practical proposition;[*A] and since in theoretical knowledge there is so much difficulty in comprehending the possibility of propositions of this kind, it may readily be gathered that in practical knowledge the difficulty will be no less.

[*The Formula of Universal Law*.]

In this task we wish first to enquire whether perhaps the mere concept of a categorical imperative may not also provide us with the formula containing the only proposition that can be a categorical imperative; for even when we know the purport of such an absolute command, the question of its possibility will still require a special and troublesome effort, which we postpone to the final chapter [not included in the present selection—Ed.].

When I conceive a *hypothetical* imperative in general, I do not know beforehand what it will contain—until its condition is given. But if I conceive a *categorical* imperative, I know at once what it contains. For since besides the law this imperative contains only the necessity that our maxim*ᴮ should conform to this law, while the law, as we have seen, contains no condition to limit it, there remains nothing over to which the maxim has to conform except the universality of a law as such; and it is this conformity alone that the imperative properly asserts to be necessary.

There is therefore only a single categorical imperative and it is this: *'Act only on that maxim through which you can at the same time will that it should become a universal law'*.

Now if all imperatives of duty can be derived from this one imperative as their principle, then even although we leave it unsettled whether what we call duty may not be an empty concept, we shall still be able to show at least what we understand by it and what the concept means.

[*The Formula of the Law of Nature.*]

Since the universality of the law governing the production of effects constitutes what is properly called *nature* in its most general sense (nature as regards its form)—that is, the existence of things so far as determined by universal laws—the universal imperative of duty may also run as follows: *'Act as if the maxim of your action were to become through your will a universal law of nature.'*

[*Illustrations.*]

We will now enumerate a few duties, following their

customary division into duties towards self and duties towards others and into perfect and imperfect duties.*c

1. A man feels sick of life as the result of misfortunes that has mounted to the point of despair, but he is still so far in possession of his reason as to ask himself whether taking his own life may not be contrary to his duty to himself. He now applies the test 'Can the maxim of my action really become a universal law of nature?' His maxim is 'From self-love I make it my principle to shorten my life if its continuance threatens more evil than it promises pleasure'. The only further question to ask is whether this principle of self-love can become a universal law of nature. It is then seen at once that a system of nature by whose law the very same feeling whose function (*Bestimmung*) is to stimulate the furtherance of life should actually destroy life would contradict itself and consequently should not subsist as a system of nature. Hence this maxim cannot possibly hold as a universal law of nature and is there fore entirely opposed to the supreme principle of all duty.

2. Another finds himself driven to borrowing money because of need. He well knows that he will not be able to pay it back; but he sees too that he will get no loan unless he gives a firm promise to pay it back within a fixed time. He is inclined to make such a promise; but he has still enough conscience to ask 'Is it not unlawful and contrary to duty to get out of difficulties in this way?' Supposing, however, he did resolve to do so, the maxim of his action would run thus: 'Whenever I believe myself short of money, I will borrow money and promise to pay it back, though I know that this will never be done'. Now this principle of self-love or personal advantage is perhaps quite compatible with my own entire future welfare; only there remains the question 'Is it right?' I

therefore transform the demand of self-love into a universal law and frame my question thus: 'How would things stand if my maxim became a universal law?' I then see straight away that this maxim can never rank as a universal law of nature and be self-consistent, but must necessarily contradict itself. For the universality of a law that every one believing himself to be in need can make any promise he pleases with the intention not to keep it would make promising, and the very purpose of promising, itself impossible, since no one would believe he was being promised anything, but would laugh at utterances of this kind as empty shams.

3. A third finds in himself a talent whose cultivation would make him a useful man for all sorts of purposes. But he sees himself in comfortable circumstances, and he prefers to give himself up to pleasure rather than to bother about increasing and improving his fortunate natural aptitudes. Yet he asks himself further 'Does my maxim of neglecting my natural gifts, besides agreeing in itself with my tendency to indulgence, agree also with what is called duty?' He then sees that a system of nature could indeed always subsist under such a universal law, although (like the South Sea Islanders) every man should let his talents rust and should be bent on devoting his life solely to idleness, indulgence, procreation, and, in a word, to enjoyment. Only he cannot possibly *will* that this should become a universal law of nature or should be implanted in us as such a law by a natural instinct. For as a rational being he necessarily wills that all his powers should be developed, since they serve him, and are given him, for all sorts of possible ends.

4. Yet a *fourth* is himself flourishing, but he sees others who have to struggle with great hardships (and whom he could easily help); and he thinks 'What does it

matter to me? Let every one be as happy as Heaven wills or as he can make himself; I won't deprive him of anything; I won't even envy him; only I have no wish to contribute anything to his well-being or to his support in distress!' Now admittedly if such an attitude were a universal law of nature, mankind could get on perfectly well—better no doubt than if everybody prates about sympathy and goodwill, and even takes pains, on occasion, to practise them, but on the other hand cheats where he can, traffics in human rights, or violates them in other ways. But although it is possible that a universal law of nature could subsist in harmony with this maxim, yet it is impossible to *will* that such a principle should hold everywhere as a law of nature. For a will which decided in this way would be in conflict with itself, since many a situation might arise in which the man needed love and sympathy from others, and in which, by such a law of nature sprung from his own will, he would rob himself of all hope of the help he wants for himself.

[*The canon of moral judgement.*]

These are some of the many actual duties—or at least of what we take to be such—whose derivation from the single principle cited above leaps to the eye. We must be *able to will* that a maxim of our action should become a universal law—this is the general canon for all moral judgement of action. Some actions are so constituted that their maxim cannot even be *conceived* as a universal law of nature without contradiction, let alone be *willed* as what *ought* to become one. In the case of others we do not find this inner impossibility, but it is still impossible to *will* that their maxim should be raised to the universality of a law of nature, because such a will would contradict itself. It is easily seen that the first kind of action is opposed to strict or narrow (rigorous) duty, the second only to wider (meritorious) duty; and thus that by these examples all duties—so far as the type of obligation is concerned (not the object of dutiful action)—are fully set out in their dependence on our single principle.

If we now attend to ourselves whenever we transgress a duty, we find that we in fact do not will that our maxim should become a universal law—since this is impossible for us—but rather that its opposite should remain a law universally; we only take the liberty of making an *exception* to it for ourselves (or even just for this once) to the advantage of our inclination. Consequently if we weighed it all up from one and the same point of view—that of reason—we should find a contradiction in our own will, the contradiction that a certain principle should be objectively necessary as a universal law and yet subjectively should not hold universally but should admit of exceptions. Since, however, we first consider our action from the point of view of a will wholly in accord with reason, and then consider precisely the same action from the point of view of a will affected by inclination, there is here actually no contradiction, but rather an opposition of inclination to the precept of reason (*antagonismus*), whereby the universality of the principle (*universalitas*) is turned into a mere generality (*generalitas*) so that the practical principle of reason may meet our maxim half-way. This procedure, though in our own impartial judgement it cannot be justified, proves none the less that we in fact recognize the validity of the categorical imperative and (with all respect for it) merely permit ourselves a few exceptions which are, as we pretend, inconsiderable and apparently forced upon us.

We have thus at least shown this much—that if duty is a concept which is to have meaning and real legislative authority for our actions, this can be expressed only in categorical imperatives and by no means in hypothetical ones. At the same time—and this is already a great deal—we have set forth distinctly, and determinately for every type of application, the content of the categorical imperative, which must contain the principle of all duty (if there is to be such a thing at all). But we are still not so far advanced as to prove *a priori* that there actually is an imperative of this kind—that there is a practical law which by itself commands absolutely and without any further motives, and that the following of this law is duty.

[*The need for pure ethics.*]

For the purpose of achieving this proof it is of the utmost importance to take warning that we should not dream for a moment of trying to derive the reality of this principle from *the special characteristics of human nature*. For duty has to be a practical, unconditioned necessity of action; it must therefore hold for all rational beings (to whom alone an imperative can apply at all), and *only because of this* can it also be a law for all human wills. Whatever, on the other hand, is derived from the special predisposition of humanity, from certain feelings and propensities, and even, if this were possible, from some special bent peculiar to human reason and not holding necessarily for the will of every rational being—all this can indeed supply a personal maxim, but not a law; it can give us a subjective principle—one on which we have a propensity and inclination to act—but not an objective one on which we should be *directed* to act although our every propensity, inclination, and natural bent were opposed to it; so much so that the sublimity and inner worth of the command is the more manifest in a duty, the fewer are the subjective causes for obeying it and the more those against—without, however, on this account weakening in the slightest the necessitation exercised by the law or detracting anything from its validity.

It is here that philosophy is seen in actual fact to be placed in a precarious position, which is supposed to be firm although neither in heaven nor on earth is there anything from which it depends or on which it is based. It is here that she has to show her purity as the authoress of her own laws—not as the mouthpiece of laws whispered to her by some implanted sense or by who knows what tutelary nature, all of which laws together, though they may always be better than nothing, can never furnish us with principles dictated by reason. These principles must have an origin entirely and completely *a priori* and must at the same time derive from this their sovereign authority—that they expect nothing from the inclinations of man, but everything from the supremacy of the law and from the reverence due to it, or in default of this condemn man to self-contempt and inward abhorrence.

Hence everything that is empirical is, as a contribution to the principle of morality, not only wholly unsuitable for the purpose, but is even highly injurious to the purity of morals; for in morals the proper worth of an absolutely good will, a worth elevated above all price, lies precisely in this—that the principle of action is free from all influence on contingent grounds, the only kind that experience can supply. Against the slack, or indeed ignoble, attitude which seeks for the moral principle among empirical motives and laws we cannot give a warning too strongly or too often; for human reason in its weariness is fain to rest upon this pillow and in a dream of sweet illusions (which lead it to embrace a

cloud in mistake for Juno) to foist into the place of
morality some misbegotten mongrel patched up from
limbs of very varied ancestry and looking like anything
you please, only not like virtue, to him who has once
beheld her in her true shape.*D

Our question therefore is this: 'Is it a necessary law
for *all rational beings* always to judge their actions by
reference to those maxims of which they can themselves
will that they should serve as universal laws?' If there is
such a law, it must already be connected (entirely *a priori*) with the concept of the will of a rational being as
such. But in order to discover this connection we must,
however much we may bristle, take a step beyond it—
that is, into metaphysics, although into a region of it different from that of speculative philosophy, namely, the
metaphysic of morals. In practical philosophy we are not
concerned with accepting reasons for what *happens*, but
with accepting laws of what *ought to happen*, even if it
never does happen—that is, objective practical laws. And
here we have no need to set up an enquiry as to the reasons why anything pleases or displeases; how the pleasure of mere sensation differs from taste, and whether
the latter differs from a universal approval by reason;
whereon feelings of pleasure and displeasure are based;
how from these feelings there arise desires and inclinations; and how from these in turn, with the co-operation
of reason, there arise maxims. All this belongs to empirical psychology, which would constitute the second part
of the doctrine of nature, if we take this doctrine to be
the *philosophy of nature* so far as grounded on *empirical
laws*. Here, however, we are discussing objective practical laws, and consequently the relation of a will to itself
as determined solely by reason. Everything related to the
empirical then falls away of itself; for if *reason entirely*

by itself determines conduct (and it is the possibility of this which we now wish to investigate), it must necessarily do so *a priori*.

[*The Formula of the End in Itself*]

The will is conceived as a power of determining oneself to action *in accordance with the idea of certain laws*. And such a power can be found only in rational beings. Now what serves the will as a subjective ground of its self-determination is an *end*; and this, if it is given by reason alone, must be equally valid for all rational beings. What, on the other hand, contains merely the ground of the possibility of an action whose effect is an end is called a *means*. The subjective ground of a desire is an *impulsion* (*Triebfeder*); the objective ground of a volition is a *motive* (*Bewegungsgrund*). Hence the difference between subjective ends, which are based on impulsions, and objective ends, which depend on motives valid for every rational being. Practical principles are *formal* if they abstract from all subjective ends; they are *material*, on the other hand, if they are based on such ends and consequently on certain impulsions. Ends that a rational being adopts arbitrarily as effects of his action (material ends) are in every case only relative; for it is solely their relation to special characteristics in the subject's power of appetition which gives them their value. Hence this value can provide no universal principles, no principles valid and necessary for all rational beings and also for every volition—that is, no practical laws. Consequently all these relative ends can be the ground only of hypothetical imperatives.

Suppose, however, there were something *whose existence* has *in itself* an absolute value, something which as *an end in itself* could be a ground of determinate laws;

then in it, and in it alone, would there be the ground of a possible categorical imperative—that is, of a practical law.

Now I say that man, and in general every rational being, *exists* as an end in himself, *not merely as a means* for an arbitrary use by this or that will: he must in all his actions, whether they are directed to himself or to other rational beings, always be viewed *at the same time as an end*. All the objects of inclination have only a conditioned value; for if there were not these inclinations and the needs grounded on them, their object would be valueless. Inclinations themselves, as sources of needs, are so far from having an absolute value to make them desirable for their own sake that it must rather be the universal wish of every rational being to be wholly free from them. Thus the value of all objects that can *be produced* by our action is always conditioned. Beings whose existence depends, not on our will, but on nature, have none the less, if they are non-rational beings, only a relative value as means and are consequently called *things*. Rational beings, on the other hand, are called *persons* because their nature already marks them out as ends in themselves—that is, as something which ought not to be used merely as a means—and consequently imposes to that extent a limit on all arbitrary treatment of them (and is an object of reverence). Persons, therefore, are not merely subjective ends whose existence as an object of our actions has a value *for us*: they are *objective ends*—that is, things whose existence is in itself an end, and indeed an end such that in its place we can put no other end to which they should serve *simply* as means; for unless this is so, nothing at all of *absolute* value would be found anywhere. But if all value were conditioned—that is, contingent—then no supreme principle could be found for reason at all.

If then there is to be a supreme practical principle and—so far as the human will is concerned—a categorical imperative, it must be such that from the idea of something which is necessarily an end for every one because it is an *end in itself* it forms an *objective* principle of the will and consequently can serve as a practical law. The ground of this principle is: *Rational nature exists as an end in itself.* This is the way in which a man necessarily conceives his own existence: it is therefore so far a *subjective* principle of human actions. But it is also the way in which every other rational being conceives his existence on the same rational ground which is valid also for me;*E hence it is at the same time an *objective* principle, from which, as a supreme practical ground, it must be possible to derive all laws for the will. The practical imperative will therefore be as follows: *Act in such a way that you always treat humanity, whether in your own person or in the person of any other, never simply as a means, but always at the same time as an end.* We will now consider whether this can be carried out in practice.

[*Illustrations.*]

Let us keep to our previous examples.

First, as regards the concept of a necessary duty to oneself, the man who contemplates suicide will ask 'Can my action be compatible with the Idea of humanity *as an end in itself?*' If he does away with himself in order to escape from a painful situation, he is making use of a person merely as a *means* to maintain a tolerable state of affairs till the end of his life. But man is not a thing—not something to be used *merely* as a means: he must always in all his actions be regarded as an end in himself. Hence I cannot dispose of man in my person by maiming, spoiling, or killing. (A more precise determination of this principle in order to avoid all misunderstanding—for example, about having limbs amputated to save myself or about exposing my life to danger in order to preserve it, and so on—I must here forego: this question belongs to morals proper.)

Secondly, so far as necessary or strict duty to others is concerned, the man who has a mind to make a false promise to others will see at once that he is intending to make use of another man *merely as a means* to an end he does not share. For the man whom I seek to use for my own purposes by such a promise cannot possibly agree with my way of behaving to him, and so cannot himself share the end of the action. This incompatibility with the principle of duty to others leaps to the eye more obviously when we bring in examples of attempts on the freedom and property of others. For then it is manifest that a violator of the rights of man intends to use the person of others merely as a means without taking into consideration that, as rational beings, they ought always at the same time to be rated as ends—that is, only as beings who must themselves be able to share in the end of the very same action.*F

Thirdly, in regard to contingent (meritorious) duty to oneself, it is not enough that an action should refrain from conflicting with humanity in our own person as an end in itself: it must also *harmonize with this end*. Now there are in humanity capacities for greater perfection which form part of nature's purpose for humanity in our person. To neglect these can admittedly be compatible with the *maintenance* of humanity as an end in itself, but not with the *promotion* of this end.

Fourthly, as regards meritorious duties to others, the natural end which all men seek is their own happiness. Now humanity could no doubt subsist if everybody contributed nothing to the happiness of others but at the same time refrained from deliberately impairing their happiness. This is, however, merely to agree negatively and not positively with *humanity as an end in itself* unless every one endeavours also, so far as in him lies, to further the ends of others. For the ends of a subject who is an end in himself must, if this conception is to have its *full* effect in me, be also, as far as possible, *my* ends.

[*The Formula of Autonomy.*]

This principle of humanity, and in general of every rational agent, *as an end in itself* (a principle which is the supreme limiting condition of every man's freedom of action) is not borrowed from experience; firstly, because it is universal, applying as it does to all rational beings as such, and no experience is adequate to determine universality; secondly, because in it humanity is conceived, not as an end of man (subjectively)—that is, as an object which, as a matter of fact, happens to be made an end—but as an objective end—one which, be our ends what they may, must, as a law, constitute the supreme limiting condition of all subjective ends and so must spring from pure reason. That is to say, the ground for every enactment of practical law lies *objectively in the rule* and in the form of universality which (according to our first principle) makes the rule capable of being a law (and indeed a law of nature); *subjectively*, however, it lies in the *end*; but (according to our second principle) the subject of all ends is to be found in every rational being as an end in himself. From this there now follows our third practical principle for the will—as the supreme condition of the will's conformity with universal practical reason—namely, the Idea of *the will of every rational being as a will which makes universal law.*

By this principle all maxims are repudiated which cannot accord with the will's own enactment of universal law. The will is therefore not merely subject to the law, but is so subject that it must be considered as also *making the law* for itself and precisely on this account as first of all subject to the law (of which it can regard itself as the author).

[*The exclusion of interest.*]

Imperatives as formulated above—namely, the imperative enjoining conformity of actions to universal law on the analogy of a *natural order* and that enjoining the universal *supremacy* of rational beings in themselves *as ends*—did, by the mere fact that they were represented as categorical, exclude from their sovereign authority every admixture of interest as a motive. They were, however, merely *assumed* to be categorical because we were bound to make this assumption if we wished to explain the concept of duty. That there were practical propositions which commanded categorically could not itself be proved, any more than it can be proved in this chapter generally; but one thing could have been done—namely, to show that in willing for the sake of duty renunciation of all interest, as the specific mark distinguishing a categorical from a hypothetical imperative, was expressed in the very imperative itself by means of some determination inherent in it. This is what is done in the present third formulation of the principle—namely, in the Idea of the will of every rational being as *a will which makes universal law.*

Once we conceive a will of this kind, it becomes clear that while a will *which is subject to law* may be bound to this law by some interest, nevertheless a will which is itself a supreme law-giver cannot possibly as such depend on any interest; for a will which is dependent in this way would itself require yet a further law in order to restrict the interest of self-love to the condition that this interest should itself be valid as a universal law.

Thus the *principle* that every human will is *a will which by all its maxims enacts universal law**G—provided only that it were right in other ways—would be *well suited* to be a categorical imperative in this respect: that precisely because of the Idea of making universal law it is *based on no interest* and consequently can alone among all possible imperatives be *unconditioned*. Or better still—to convert the proposition—if there is a categorical imperative (that is, a law for the will of every rational being), it can command us only to act always on the maxim of such a will in us as can at the same time look upon itself as making universal law; for only then is the practical principle and the imperative which we obey unconditioned, since it is wholly impossible for it to be based on any interest.

We need not now wonder, when we look back upon all the previous efforts that have been made to discover the principle of morality, why they have one and all been bound to fail. Their authors saw man as tied to laws by his duty, but it never occurred to them that he is subject only to *laws which are made by himself* and yet are *universal*, and that he is bound only to act in conformity with a will which is his own but has as nature's purpose for it the function of making universal law. For when they thought of man merely as subject to a law (whatever it might be), the law had to carry with it some interest in order to attract or compel, because it did not spring as a law from *his own* will: in order to conform with the law his will had to be necessitated by *something else* to act in a certain way. This absolutely inevitable conclusion meant that all the labour spent in trying to find a supreme principle of duty was lost beyond recall; for what they discovered was never duty, but only the necessity of acting from a certain interest. This interest might be one's own or another's; but on such a view the imperative was bound to be always a conditioned one and could not possibly serve as a moral law. I will therefore call my principle the principle of the *Autonomy* of the will in contrast with all others, which I consequently class under *Heteronomy*.

[*The Formula of the Kingdom of Ends*.]

The concept of every rational being as one who must regard himself as making universal law by all the maxims of his will, and must seek to judge himself and his actions from this point of view, leads to a closely connect and very fruitful concept—namely, that of *a kingdom of ends*.

I understand by a '*kingdom*' a systematic union of different rational beings under common laws. Now since laws determine ends as regards their universal validity, we shall be able—if we abstract from the personal differences between rational beings, and also from all the content of their private ends—to conceive a whole of all ends in systematic conjunction (a whole both of rational beings as ends in themselves and also of the personal ends which each may set before himself); that is, we shall be able to conceive a kingdom of ends which is possible in accordance with the above principles.

For rational beings all stand under the *law* that each of them should treat himself and all others, *never merely as a means*, but *always at the same time as an end in himself*. But by so doing there arises a systematic union of rational beings under common objective laws—that is, a kingdom. Since these laws are directed precisely to the relation of such beings to one another as ends and means, this kingdom can be called a kingdom of ends (which is admittedly only an Ideal).

A rational being belongs to the kingdom of ends as a *member*, when, although he makes its universal laws, he is also himself subject to these laws. He belongs to it as its *head*, when as the maker of laws he is himself subject to the will of no other.

A rational being must always regard himself as making laws in a kingdom of ends which is possible through freedom of the will—whether it be as member or as head. The position of the latter he can maintain, not in virtue of the maxim of his will alone, but only if he is a completely independent being, without needs and with an unlimited power adequate to his will.

Thus morality consists in the relation of all action to the making of laws whereby alone a kingdom of ends is possible. This making of laws must be found in every rational being himself and must be able to spring from his will. The principle of his will is therefore never to perform an action except on a maxim such as can also be a universal law, and consequently such *that the will can regard itself as at the same time making universal law by means of its maxim*. Where maxims are not already by their very nature in harmony with this objective principle of rational beings as makers of universal law, the necessity of acting on this principle is practical necessitation—that is, *duty*. Duty does not apply to the head in a kingdom of ends, but it does apply to every member and to all members in equal measure.

The practical necessity of acting on this principle—that is, duty—is in no way based on feelings, impulses, and inclinations, but only on the relation of rational beings to one another, a relation in which the will of a rational being must always be regarded as *making universal law*, because otherwise he could not be conceived as *an end in himself*. Reason thus relates every maxim of the will, considered as making universal law, to every other will and also to every action towards oneself: it does so, not because of any further motive or future advantage, but from the Idea of the *dignity* of a rational being who obeys no law other than that which he at the same time enacts himself.

[*The dignity of virtue.*]

In the kingdom of ends everything has either a *price* or a *dignity*. If it has a price, something else can be put in its place as an *equivalent*; if it is exalted above all price and so admits of no equivalent, then it has a dignity.

What is relative to universal human inclinations and needs has a *market price*; what, even without presupposing a need, accords with a certain taste—that is, with satisfaction in the mere purposeless play of our mental powers—has a *fancy price* (*Affektionspreis*); but that which constitutes the sole condition under which anything can be an end in itself has not merely a relative value—that is, a price—but has an intrinsic value—that is, a *dignity*.

Now morality is the only condition under which a rational being can be an end in himself; for only through this is it possible to be a law-making member in a kingdom of ends. Therefore morality, and humanity so far as it is capable of morality, is the only thing which has dignity. Skill and diligence in work have a market price; but fidelity to promises and kindness based on principle (not on instinct) have an intrinsic worth. In default of these, nature and art alike contain nothing to put in their place;

for their worth consists, not in the effects which result from them, not in the advantage or profit they produce, but in the attitudes of mind—that is, in the maxims of the will—which are ready in this way to manifest themselves in action even if they are not favoured by success. Such actions too need no recommendation from any subjective disposition or taste in order to meet with immediate favour and approval; they need no immediate propensity or feeling for themselves; they exhibit the will which performs them as an object of immediate reverence; nor is anything other than reason required to *impose* them upon the will, not to *coax* them from the will—which last would anyhow be a contradiction in the case of duties. This assessment reveals as dignity the value of such a mental attitude and puts it infinitely above all price, with which it cannot be brought into reckoning or comparison without, as it were, a profanation of its sanctity.

What is it then that entitles a morally good attitude of mind—or virtue—to make claims so high? It is nothing less than the *share* which it affords to a rational being *in the making of universal law*, and which therefore fits him to be a member in a possible kingdom of ends. For this he was already marked out in virtue of his own proper nature as an end in himself and consequently as a maker of laws in the kingdom of ends—as free in respect of all laws of nature, obeying only those laws which he makes himself and in virtue of which his maxims can have their part in the making of universal law (to which he at the same time subjects himself). For nothing can have a value other than that determined for it by the law. But the law-making which determines all value must for this reason have a dignity—that is, an unconditioned and incomparable worth—for the appreciation of which, as necessarily given by a rational being, the word '*rever-*

ence' is the only becoming expression. *Autonomy* is therefore the ground of the dignity of human nature and of every rational nature.

[*Review of the Formulae.*]

The aforesaid three ways of representing the principle of morality are at bottom merely so many formulations of precisely the same law, one of them by itself containing a combination of the other two. There is nevertheless a difference between them, which, however, is subjectively rather than objectively practical: that is to say, its purpose is to bring an Idea of reason nearer to intuition (in accordance with a certain analogy) and so nearer to feeling. All maxims have, in short,

1. a *form*, which consists in their universality; and in this respect the formula of the moral imperative is expressed thus: 'Maxims must be chosen as if they had to hold as universal laws of nature';

2. a *matter*—that is, an end; and in this respect the formula says: 'A rational being, as by his very nature an end and consequently an end in himself, must serve for every maxim as a condition limiting all merely relative and arbitrary ends';

3. a *complete determination* of all maxims by the following formula, namely: 'All maxims as proceeding from our own making of law ought to harmonize with a possible kingdom of ends as a kingdom of nature'.*H This progression may be said to take place through the categories of the *unity* of the form of will (its universality); of the *multiplicity* of its matter (its objects—that is, its ends); and of the *totality* or completeness of its system of ends. It is, however, better if in moral *judgement* we proceed always in accordance with the strictest method and take as our basis the universal formula of the categorical

imperative: *'Act on the maxim which can at the same time be made a universal law'*. If, however, we wish also to secure acceptance for the moral law, it is very useful to bring one and the same action under the above-mentioned three concepts and, so far as we can, to bring the universal formula nearer to intuition.

[*Review of the whole argument.*]

We can now end at the point from which we started out at the beginning—namely, the concept of an unconditionally good will. The *will* is *absolutely good* if it cannot be evil—that is, if its maxim, when made into a universal law, can never be in conflict with itself. This principle is therefore also its supreme law: 'Act always on that maxim whose universality as a law you can at the same time will'. This is the one principle on which a will can never be in conflict with itself, and such an imperative is categorical. Because the validity of the will as a universal law for possible actions is analogous to the universal interconnexion of existent things in accordance with universal laws—which constitutes the formal aspect of nature as such—we can also express the categorical imperative as follows: *'Act on that maxim which can at the same time have for its object itself as a universal law of nature'*. In this way we provide the formula for an absolutely good will.

Rational nature separates itself out from all other things by the fact that it sets itself an end. An end would thus be the matter of every good will. But in the Idea of a will which is absolutely good—good without any qualifying condition (namely, that it should attain this or that end)—there must be complete abstraction from every end that has to be *produced* (as something which would make every will only relatively good). Hence the end must here be conceived, not as an end to be produced, *but as a self-existent* end. It must therefore be conceived only negatively—that is, as an end against which we should never act, and consequently as one which in all our willing we must never rate *merely* as a means, but always at the same time as an end. Now this end can be nothing other than the subject of all possible ends himself, because this subject is also the subject of a will that may be absolutely good; for such a will cannot without contradiction be subordinated to any other object. The principle 'So act in relation to every rational being (both to yourself and to others) that he may at the same time count in your maxim as an end in himself' is thus at bottom the same as the principle 'Act on a maxim which at the same time contains in itself its own universal validity for every rational being'. For to say that in using means to every end I ought to restrict my maxim to the condition that it should also be universally valid as a law for every subject is just the same as to say this—that a subject of ends, namely a rational being himself, must be made the ground of all maxims of action, never *merely* as a means, but as a supreme condition restricting the use of every means—that is, always also as an end.

Now from this it unquestionably follows that every rational being, as an end in himself, must be able to regard himself as also the maker of universal law in respect of any law whatever to which he may be subjected; for it is precisely the fitness of his maxims to make universal law that marks him out as an end in himself. It follows equally that this dignity (or prerogative) of his above all the mere things of nature carries with it the necessity of always choosing his maxims from the point of view of himself—and also of every other rational being—as a maker of law (and this is why they are called persons). It is in this way that a world of rational beings (*mundus intelligibilis*) is possible as a kingdom of ends—possible, that is, through the making of their own laws by all persons as its member. Accordingly every rational being must so act as if he were through his maxims always a law-making member in the universal kingdom of ends. The formal principle of such maxims is 'So act as if your maxim had to serve at the same time as a universal law (for all rational beings)'. Thus a kingdom of ends is possible only on the analogy of a kingdom of nature; yet the kingdom of ends is possible only through maxims—that is, self-imposed rules—while nature is possible only through laws concerned with causes whose action is necessitated from without. In spite of this difference, we give to nature as a whole, even although it is regarded as a machine, the name of a 'kingdom of nature' so far as—and for the reason that—it stands in a relation to rational beings as its ends. Now a kingdom of ends would actually come into existence through maxims which the categorical imperative prescribes as a rule for all rational beings, *if these maxims were universally followed.* Yet even if a rational being were himself to follow such a maxim strictly, he cannot count on everybody else being faithful to it on this ground, nor can he be confident that the kingdom of nature and its purposive order will work in harmony with him, as a fitting member, towards a kingdom of ends made possible by himself—or, in other words, that it will favour his expectation of happiness. But in spite of this the law 'Act on the maxims of a member who makes universal laws for a merely possible kingdom of ends' remains in full force, since its command is categorical. And precisely here we encounter the paradox that without any further end or advantage to be attained the mere dignity of humanity, that is, of rational nature in man—and consequently that reverence for a mere Idea—should function as an inflexible precept for the will; and that it is just this freedom from dependence on interested motives which constitutes the sublimity of a maxim and the worthiness of every rational subject to be a law-making member in the kingdom of ends; for otherwise he would have to be regarded as subject only to the law of nature—the law of his own needs. Even if it were thought that both the kingdom of nature and the kingdom of ends were united under one head and that thus the latter kingdom ceased to be a mere Idea and genuine reality, the Idea would indeed gain by this the addition of a strong motive, but never any increase in its intrinsic worth; for, even if this were so, it would still be necessary to conceive the unique and absolute law-giver himself as judging the worth of rational beings solely by the disinterested behaviour they prescribed to themselves in virtue of this Idea alone. The essence of things does not vary with their external relations; and where there is something which, without regard to such relations, constitutes by itself the absolute worth of man, it is by this that man must also be judged by everyone whatsoever—even by the Supreme Being. Thus *morality* lies in the relation of actions to the autonomy of the will—that is, to a possible making of universal law by means of its maxims. An action which is compatible with the autonomy of the will is *permitted*; one which does not harmonize with it is *forbidden*. A will whose maxims necessarily accord with the laws of autonomy is a *holy*, or absolutely good, will. The dependence of a will not absolutely good on the principle of autonomy (that is, moral necessitation) is *obligation*. Obligation can thus have no reference to a holy being. The objective necessity to act from obligation is called *duty*.

From what was said a little time ago we can now easily explain how it comes about that, although in the concept of duty we think of subjection to the law, yet we also at the same time attribute to the person who fulfils all his duties a certain sublimity and *dignity*. For it is not in so far as he is *subject* to the law that he has sublimity, but rather in so far as, in regard to this very same law, he is at the same time its *author* and is subordinated to it only on this ground. We have also shown above how neither fear nor inclination, but solely reverence for the law, is the motive which can give an action moral worth. Our own will, provided it were to act only under the condition of being able to make universal law by means of its maxims—this ideal will which can be ours is the proper object of reverence; and the dignity of man consists precisely in his capacity to make universal law, although only on condition of being himself also subject to the law he makes.

AUTONOMY OF THE WILL
as the supreme principle of morality.

Autonomy of the will is the property the will has of being a law to itself (independently of every property belonging to the objects of volition). Hence the principle of autonomy is 'Never to choose except in such a way that in the same volition the maxims of your choice are also present as universal law'. That this practical rule is an imperative—that is, that the will of every rational being is necessarily bound to the rule as a condition—cannot be proved by mere analysis of the concepts contained in it, since it is a synthetic proposition. For proof we should have to go beyond knowledge of objects and pass to a critique of the subject—that is, of pure practical reason—since this synthetic proposition, as commanding apodeictically, must be capable of being known entirely *a priori*. This task does not belong to the present chapter. None the less by mere analysis of the concepts of morality we can quite well show that the above principle of autonomy is the sole principle of ethics. For analysis finds that the principle of morality must be a categorical imperative, and that this in turn commands nothing more nor less than precisely this autonomy.

HETERONOMY OF THE WILL
as the source of all spurious principles of morality.

If the will seeks the law that is to determine it *anywhere else* than in the fitness of its maxims for its own making of universal law—if therefore in going beyond itself it seeks this law in the character of any of its objects—the result is always *heteronomy*. In that case the will does not give itself the law, but the object does so in virtue of its relation to the will. This relation, whether based on inclination or on rational ideas, can give rise only to hypothetical imperatives: 'I ought to do something *because I will something else*'. As against this, the moral, and therefore categorical, imperative says: 'I ought to will thus or thus, although I have not willed something else'. For example, the first says: 'I ought not to lie if I want to maintain my reputation'; while the second says: 'I ought not to lie even if so doing were to bring me not the slightest disgrace'. The second imperative must therefore abstract from all objects to this extent—they should be without any *influence* at all on the will so that practical reason (the will) may not merely administer an alien interest but may simply manifest its own sovereign authority as the supreme maker of law. Thus, for example, the reason why I ought to promote the happiness of others is not because the realization of their happiness is of consequence to myself (whether on account of immediate inclination or on account of some satisfaction gained indirectly through reason), but solely because a maxim which excludes this cannot also be present in one and the same volition as a universal law.

---

*A Without presupposing a condition taken from some inclination I connect an action with the will *a priori* and therefore necessarily (although only objectively so—that is, only subject to the Idea of a reason having full power over all subjective impulses to action). Here we have a practical proposition in which the willing of an action is not derived analytically from some other willing already presupposed (for we do not possess any such perfect will), but is on the contrary connected immediately with the concept of the will of a rational being as something which is not contained in this concept.

*B A *maxim* is a subjective principle of action and must be distinguished from an *objective principle*—namely, a practical law. The former contains a practical rule determined by reason in accordance with the conditions of the subject (often his ignorance or again his inclinations): it is thus a principle on which the subject *acts*. A law, on the other hand, is an objective principle valid for every rational being; and it is a principle on which he *ought to act*—that is, an imperative.

*C It should be noted that I reserve my division of duties entirely for a future *Metaphysic of Morals* and that my present division is therefore put forward as arbitrary (merely for the purpose of arranging my examples). Further, I understand here by a perfect duty one which allows no exception in the interests of inclination, and so I recognize among *perfect duties*, not only outer ones, but also inner. This is contrary to the accepted usage of the schools, but I do not intend to justify it here, since for my purpose it is all one whether this point is conceded or not.

•D To behold virtue in her proper shape is nothing other than to show morality stripped of all admixture with the sensuous and of all the spurious adornments of reward or self-love. How much she then casts into the shade all else that appears attractive to the inclinations can be readily perceived by every man if he will exert his reason in the slightest—provided he has not entirely ruined it for all abstractions.

•E This proposition I put forward here as a postulate. The grounds for it will be found in the final chapter [not included in the present selection—Ed.].

•F Let no one think that here the trivial '*quod tibi non vis fieri, etc.*' can serve as a standard or principle. For it is merely derivative from our principle, although subject to various qualifications: it cannot be a universal law since it contains the ground neither of duties to oneself nor of duties of kindness to others (for many a man would readily agree that others should not help him if only he could be dispensed from affording help to them), nor finally of strict duties towards others; for on this basis the criminal would be able to dispute with the judges who punish him, and so on.

•G I may be excused from bringing forward samples to illustrate this principle, since those which were first used as illustrations of the categorical imperative and its formula can all serve this purpose here.

•H Teleology views nature as a kingdom of ends; ethics view a possible kingdom of ends as a kingdom of nature. In the first case the kingdom of ends is a theoretical Idea used to explain what exists. In the second case it is a practical Idea used to bring into existence what does not exist but can be made actual by our conduct—and indeed to bring it into existence in conformity with this Idea .

Critique of Practical Reason

tr. Lewis White Beck.
New York: Bobbs-Merrill, 1958

(pp. 30–40)

§.7 *Fundamental Law of Pure Practical Reason*

So act that the maxim of your will could always hold at the same time as a principle establishing universal law.

REMARK

Pure geometry has postulates as practical propositions, which, however, contain nothing more than the presupposition that one *can* do something and that, when some result is needed, one *should* do it; these are the only propositions of pure geometry which apply to an existing thing. They are thus practical rules under a problematic condition of the will. Here, however, the rule says: One ought absolutely to act in a certain way. The practical rule is therefore unconditional and thus is thought of a priori as a categorically practical proposition. The practical rule, which is thus here a law, absolutely and directly determines the will objectively, for pure reason, practical in itself, is here directly legislative. The will is thought of as independent of empirical conditions and consequently as pure will, determined by the mere form of the law, and this ground of determination is regarded as the supreme condition of all maxims.

The thing is strange enough and has no parallel in the remainder of practical knowledge. For the a priori thought of the possibility of giving universal law, which is thus merely problematic, is unconditionally commanded as a law without borrowing anything from experience or from any external will. It is, however, not a prescription according to which an act should occur in order to make a desired effect possible, for such a rule is always physically conditioned; it is, on the contrary, a rule which determines the will a priori only with respect to the form of its maxims. Therefore, it is at least not impossible to conceive of a law which merely serves the purpose of the *subjective* form of principles and yet is a ground of determination by virtue of the *objective* form of a law in general. The consciousness of this fundamental law may be called a fact of reason, since one cannot ferret it out from antecedent data of reason, such as the consciousness of freedom (for this is not antecedently given), and since it forces itself upon us as a synthetic proposition a priori based on no pure or empirical intuition. It would be analytic if the freedom of the will were presupposed, but for this, as a positive concept, an intellectual intuition would be needed, and here we cannot assume it. In order to regard this law without any misinterpretation as given, one must note that it is not an empirical fact but the sole fact of pure reason, which by it proclaims itself as originating law (*sic volo, sic iubeo*).

COROLLARY

Pure reason is practical of itself alone, and it gives (to man) a universal law, which we call the *moral law*.

REMARK

The fact just mentioned is undeniable. One need only analyze the sentence which men pass upon the lawfulness of their actions to see in every case that their reason, incorruptible and self-constrained, in every action holds up the maxim of the will to the pure will, i.e., to itself regarded as a priori practical; and this it does regardless of what inclination may say to the contrary. Now this principle of morality, on account of the universality of its legislation which makes it the formal supreme determining ground of the will regardless of any subjective differences among men, is declared by reason to be a law for all rational beings in so far as they have a will, i.e., faculty of determining their causality through the conception of a rule, and consequently in so far as they are competent to determine their actions according to principles and thus to act according to practical a priori principles, which alone have the necessity which reason demands in a principle. It is thus not limited to human beings but extends to all finite beings having reason and will; indeed, it includes the Infinite Being as the supreme intelligence. In the former case, however, the law has the form of an imperative. For though we can suppose that men as rational beings have a pure will, since they are affected by wants and sensuous motives we cannot suppose them to have a holy will, a will incapable of any maxims which conflict with the moral law. The moral law for them, therefore, is an imperative, commanding categorically because it is unconditioned. The relation of such a will to this law is one of dependence under the name of "obligation." This term applies a constraint to an action, though this constraint is only that of reason and its objective law. Such an action is called *duty*, because a pathologically affected (though not pathologically determined—and thus still free) choice involves a wish arising from subjective causes, and consequently such a choice often opposes pure objective grounds of determination. Such a will is therefore in need of the moral constraint of the resistance offered by the practical reason, which may be called an inner but intellectual compulsion. In the supremely self-sufficing intelligence choice is correctly thought of as incapable of any maxim which could not at the same time be objectively a law, and the concept of holiness, which is applied to it for this reason, elevates it not indeed above all practical laws but above all practically restrictive laws, and thus above obligation and duty. This holiness of will is, however, a practical ideal which must necessarily serve as a model which all finite rational beings must strive toward even though they cannot reach it. The pure moral law, which is itself for this reason called holy, constantly and rightly holds it before their eyes. The utmost that finite practical reason can accomplish is to make sure of the unending progress of its maxims toward this model and of the constancy of the finite rational being in making continuous progress. This is virtue, and, as a naturally acquired faculty, it can never be perfect, because assurance in such a case never becomes apodictic certainty, and as a mere opinion it is very dangerous.

§.8 *Theorem IV*

The *autonomy* of the will is the sole principle of all moral laws and of the duties conforming to them; *heteronomy* of choice, on the other hand, not only does not establish any obligation but is opposed to the principle of duty and to the morality of the will.

The sole principle of morality consists in independence from all material of the law (i.e., a desired object) and in the accompanying determination of choice by the mere form of giving universal law which a maxim must be capable of having. That independence, however, is freedom in the negative sense, while this intrinsic legislation of pure and thus practical reason is freedom in the positive sense. Therefore, the moral law expresses nothing else than the autonomy of the pure practical reason, i.e., freedom. This autonomy or freedom is itself the formal condition of all maxims, under which alone they can all agree with the supreme practical law. If, therefore, the material of volition, which cannot be other than an object of a desire which is connected to the law, comes into the practical law *as a condition of its possibility*, there results heteronomy of choice, or dependence on natural laws in following some impulse or inclination; it is heteronomy because the will does not give itself the law but only directions for a reasonable obedience to pathological laws. The maxim, however, which for this reason can never contain in itself the form of prescribing universal law, not only produces no obligation but is itself opposed to the principle of a pure practical reason and thus also to the moral disposition, even when the action which comes from it conforms to the law.

REMARK 1

Thus a practical precept which supposes a material and therefore empirical condition must never be reckoned a practical law. For the law of pure will, which is free, puts the will in a sphere entirely different from the empirical, and the necessity which it expresses, not being a natural necessity, can consist only in the formal conditions of the possibility of a law in general. All the material of practical rules rests only on subjective conditions, which can afford the rules no universality for rational beings (except a merely conditioned one as in the case where I desire this or that, and then there is something which I must do in order to make it real). Without exception, they all revolve about the principle of one's own happiness. Now it is certainly undeniable that every volition must have an object and therefore a material; but the material cannot be supposed, for this reason, to be the determining ground and condition of the maxim. If it were, the maxim could not be presented as giving universal law, because then the expectation of the existence of the object would be the determining cause of the choice, the dependence of the faculty of desire on the existence of some thing would have to be made basic to volition, and this dependence would have to be sought out in empirical conditions and therefore never could be a foundation of a necessary and universal rule. Thus the happiness of others may be the object of the will of a rational being, but if it were the determining ground of the maxim, not only would one have to presuppose that we find in the welfare of others a natural satisfaction but also one would have to find a want such as that which is occasioned in some men by a sympathetic disposition. This want, however, I cannot presuppose in every rational being, certainly not in God. The material of the maxim can indeed remain but cannot be its condition, for then it would not be fit for a law. The mere form of the law, which limits its material, must be a condition for adding this material to the will but not presuppose it as the condition of the will. Let the material content be, for example, my own happiness. If I attribute this to everyone, as in fact I may attribute it to all finite beings, it can become an objective practical law only if I include within it the happiness of others. Therefore, the law that we should further the happiness of others arises not from the presupposition that this law is an object of everyone's choice but from the fact that the form of universality, which reason requires as condition for giving to the maxim of self-love the objective validity of law, is itself the determining ground of the will. Therefore not the object, i.e., the happiness of others, was the determining ground of the pure will but rather it was the lawful form alone. Through it I restricted my maxim, founded on inclination, by giving it the universality of a law, thus making it conformable to the pure practical reason. From this limitation alone, and not from the addition of any external incentive, the concept of obligation arises to extend the maxim of self-love also to the happiness of others.

REMARK II

When one's own happiness is made the determining ground of the will, the result is the direct opposite of the principle of morality; and I have previously shown that, whenever the determining ground which is to serve as a law is located elsewhere than in the legislative form of the maxim, we have to reckon with this result. This conflict is not, however, merely logical, as is that between empirically conditioned rules which someone might nevertheless wish to erect into necessary principles of knowledge; it is rather a practical conflict, and, were the voice of reason with respect to the will not so distinct, so irrepressible, and so clearly audible to even the commonest man, it would drive morality to ruin. But it can only maintain itself in the perplexing speculations of the schools which are audacious enough to close their ears to that heavenly voice in order to uphold a theory that costs no brainwork.

Suppose that an acquaintance whom you otherwise liked were to attempt to justify himself before you for having borne false witness by appealing to what he regarded as the holy duty of consulting his own happiness and, then, by recounting all the advantages he had gained thereby, pointing out the prudence he had shown in securing himself against detection, even by yourself, to whom alone he now reveals the secret only in order that he may be able at any time to deny it. And suppose that he then affirmed, in all seriousness, that he had thereby fulfilled a true human duty—you would either laugh in his face or shrink from him in disgust, even though you would not have the least grounds for objecting to such measures if a man regulated his principles solely with a view to his own advantage. Or suppose someone recommends to you as steward a man to whom you could blindly trust your affairs and, in order to inspire you with confidence, further extols him as a prudent man who has a masterly understanding of his own interest and is so indefatigably active that he misses no opportunity to further it; furthermore, lest you should be afraid of finding a vulgar selfishness in him, he praises the good taste with which he lives, not seeking his pleasure in making money or in coarse wantonness, but in the increase of his knowledge, in instructive conversation with a select circle, and even in relieving the needy. But, he adds, he is not particular as to the means (which, of course, derive their value only from the end), being as willing to use another's money and property as his own, provided only that he knows that he can so safely and without discovery. You would believe that the person making such a recommendation was either mocking you or had lost his mind. So distinct and sharp are the boundaries between morality and self-love that even the commonest eye cannot distinguish whether a thing belongs to one or the other. The few remarks which follow may appear superfluous where the truth is so obvious, but they serve at least to furnish somewhat greater distinctness to the judgment of common sense.

The principle of happiness can indeed give maxims, but never maxims which are competent to be laws of the will, even if universal happiness were made the subject. For, since the knowledge of this rests on mere data of experience, as each judgment concerning it depends very much on the very changeable opinion of each person, it can give general but never universal rules; that is, the rules it gives will on the average be most often the right ones for this purpose, but they will not be rules which must hold always and necessarily. Consequently, no practical laws can be based on this principle. Since here an object of choice is made the basis of the rule and therefore must precede it, the rule cannot be founded upon or related to anything other than what one approves; and thus it refers to and is based on experience. Hence the variety of judgement must be infinite. This principle, therefore, does not prescribe the same practical rules to all rational beings, even though all the rules go under the same name—that of happiness. The moral law, however, is thought of as objectively necessary only because it holds good for everyone having reason and will.

The maxim of self-love (prudence) merely advises; the law of morality commands. Now there is a great difference between that which we are advised to do and that which we are obligated to do.

What is required in accordance with the principle of autonomy of choice is easily and without hesitation seen by the commonest intelligence; what is to be done under the presupposition of its heteronomy is hard to see and requires knowledge of the world. That is to say, what duty is, is plain of itself to everyone, but what is to bring true, lasting advantage to our whole existence is veiled in impenetrable obscurity, and much prudence is required to adapt the practical rule based upon it even tolerably to the ends of life by making suitable exceptions to it. But even the moral law commands the most unhesitating obedience from everyone; consequently, the decision as to what is to be done in accordance with it must not be so difficult that even the commonest and most unpracticed understanding without any worldly prudence should go wrong in making it.

It is always in everyone's power to satisfy the commands of the categorical command of morality; this is but seldom possible with respect to the empirically conditioned precept of happiness, and it is far from being possible, even in respect to a single purpose, for everyone. The reason is that in the former it is only a question of the maxim, which must be genuine and pure, but in the latter it is also a question of capacity and physical ability to realize a desired object. A command that everyone should seek to make himself happy would be foolish, for no one commands another to do what he already invariably wishes to do. One must only command—or better, provide—the means to him, since he cannot do everything which he wishes. But to command morality under the name of duty is very reasonable, for its precept will not, for one thing, be willingly obeyed by everyone when it is in conflict with his inclinations. Then, regarding the means of obeying this law, there is no need to teach them, for in this respect whatever he wills to do he also can do.

He who has lost at play may be vexed at himself

and his imprudence; but when he is conscious of having cheated at play, even though he has won, he must despise himself as soon as he compares himself with the moral law. This must therefore be something else than the principle of one's own happiness. For to have to say to himself, "I am a worthless man, though I've filled my purse," he must have a different criterion of judgment than if he approves and says, "I am a prudent man, for I've enriched my treasure."

Finally, there is something else in the idea of our practical reason which accompanies transgression of a moral law, namely, its culpability. Becoming a partaker in happiness cannot be united with the concept of punishment as such. For even though he who punishes can do so with the benevolent intention of directing this punishment to this end, it must nevertheless be justified as punishment, i.e., as mere harm in itself, so that even the punished person, if it stopped there and he could see no glimpse of kindness behind the harshness, would yet have to admit that justice had been done and that his reward perfectly fitted his behavior. In every punishment as such there must first be justice, and this constitutes the essence of the concept. With it benevolence may, of course, be associated, but the person who deserves punishment has not the least reason to count on it. Punishment is physical harm which, even if not bound as a natural consequence to the morally bad, ought to be bound as a natural consequence according to principles of moral legislation. Now if every crime, without regard to the physical consequences to him who commits it, is punishable, i.e., involves a forfeiture of happiness at least in part, it is obviously absurd to say that the crime consists just in the fact that one has brought punishment upon himself and thus has injured his own happiness (which, according to the principle of self-love, must be the correct concept of all crime). In this way, the punishment would be the reason for calling anything a crime, and justice would consist in withholding all punishment and even hindering natural punishment, for there would be no longer any evil in an action, since the harm which would otherwise follow upon it and because of which alone the action was called bad would now be omitted. To look upon all punishment and reward as machinery in the hand of a higher power, which by this means sets rational beings in action toward their final purpose (happiness), so obviously reduces the will to a mechanism destructive of freedom that it need not detain us.

More refined, but equally untrue, is the pretense of those who assume a certain particular moral sense which, instead of reason, determines the moral law, and in accordance with which the consciousness of virtue is directly associated with satisfaction and enjoyment, while consciousness of vice is associated with mental restlessness and pain. Thus everything is reduced to the desire for one's own happiness. Without repeating what has already been said, I will only indicate the fallacy they fall into. In order to imagine the vicious person as tormented with mortification by the consciousness of his transgressions, they must presuppose that he is, in the core of his character, at least to a certain degree morally good, just as they have to think of the person who is delighted by the consciousness of doing dutiful acts as already virtuous. Therefore, the concept of morality and duty must precede all reference to this satisfaction and cannot be derived from it. One must already value the importance of what we call duty, the respect for the moral law, and the immediate worth which a person obtains in his own eyes through obedience to it, in order to feel satisfaction in the consciousness of his conformity to law or the bitter remorse which accompanies his awareness that he has transgressed it. Therefore, this satisfaction or spiritual unrest cannot be felt prior to the knowledge of obligation, nor can it be made the basis of the latter. One must be at least halfway honest even to be able to have an idea of these feelings. For the rest, as the human will by virtue of its freedom is directly determined by the moral law, I am far from denying that frequent practice in accordance with this determining ground can itself finally cause a subjective feeling of satisfaction. Indeed, it is a duty to establish and cultivate this feeling, which alone deserves to be called the moral feeling. But the concept of duty cannot be derived from it, for we would have to presuppose a feeling for law as such and regard as an object of sensation what can only be thought by reason. If this did not end up in the flattest contradiction, it would destroy every concept of duty and fill its place with a merely mechanical play of refined inclinations, sometimes contending with the coarser.

The Doctrine of Virtue

tr. Mary J. Gregor.
New York: Harper and Row,
1964

(pp. 36–51)

INTRODUCTION
to the Doctrine of Virtue

I.

EXPOSITION OF THE CONCEPT OF A DOCTRINE OF VIRTUE

The *concept of duty* as such is the notion of a *necessitation* (constraint) of *free* choice by the law; this constraint may be either *external* compulsion or *self-*constraint. The moral *imperative* announces this constraint by its categorical dictum (the unconditioned *Ought*). Hence the constraint does not refer to rational beings as such (there might be *holy* ones) but rather to *men*, *natural* beings endowed with reason who are unholy enough that pleasure can induce them to transgress the moral law, even though they recognize its authority. And when they do obey the law, they do it *reluctantly* (in the face of opposition from their inclinations), and so under *constraint*.*a But since man is still a free (moral) being, when the concept of duty concerns the inner determination of his choice (the motive), the constraint which duty contains can be only self-constraint (by the mere thought of the law); for only so can freedom of choice be reconciled with that necessitation (even if it be external). Hence in this case the concept of duty will be an ethical one.

The impulses of nature, accordingly, are *obstacles* within man's mind to his observance of duty and forces (sometimes powerful ones) struggling against it. Man must, therefore, judge that he is able to stand up to them and subdue them by reason—not at some time in the future but at once (the moment he thinks of duty): he must judge that he *can* do what the law commands unconditionally that he *ought* to do.

Now the power and deliberate resolve to withstand a strong but unjust opponent is *fortitude* (*fortitudo*); and fortitude in relation to the forces opposing a moral attitude of will *in us* is virtue (*virtus, fortitudo moralis*). So the part of the general doctrine of duties that brings inner, rather than outer, freedom under laws is a *doctrine of virtue*.

The doctrine of Law deals only with the *formal* condition of outer freedom (the consistency of outer freedom with itself if its maxim were made universal law)—that is, with Law. But ethics goes beyond this and provides a *matter* (an object of free choice) an end of pure reason which it presents also as an objectively necessary end, *i.e.* an end which, so far as men are concerned, it is a duty to have.—For since the sensuous inclinations tempt us to ends (as the matter of choice) which may be contrary to duty, legislative reason can check their influence only by another end, a moral end set up against the ends of inclination, which must therefore be given *a priori*, independently of the inclinations.

An *end* is an object of the power of choice (of a rational being), through the thought of which choice is determined to an action to produce this object. —Now another person can indeed compel me to perform actions which are means to his end, but he cannot compel me to *have an end*; only I myself can make something my end. —But the notion that I am under obligation to take as my end something that lies in the concepts of practical reason, and so to have a material determining ground of choice beyond the formal one that Law contains, would be the concept of *an end which is in itself a duty*. The doctrine of this end would not belong to the doctrine of Law but rather to ethics, since the concept of *self-constraint* in accordance with moral laws belongs only to ethics.

For this reason ethics can also be defined as the system of the *ends* of pure practical reason. —Ends and duties [to which we can be compelled by others] differentiate the two divisions of moral philosophy in general. That ethics contains duties which others cannot compel us (by natural means) to fulfill is merely the consequence of its being a doctrine of *ends*; for compulsion to have or to adopt ends is self-contradictory.

That ethics is a *doctrine of virtue* (*doctrina officiorum virtutis*—[doctrine of the offices of virtue]) follows from the above definition of virtue when we connect it with the kind of obligation proper to ethics. —Determination to an *end* is the only determination of choice which in its very concept excludes the possibility of compulsion *through natural means* by another's *act of choice*. Another can indeed *compel* me to do something that is not my end (but only a means to his end), but he cannot compel me *to make it my end*. To have an end that I have not myself made an end would be a self-contradiction—

an act of freedom which is still not free. —But it is no contradiction that I myself set an end which is also a duty, since I constrain myself to it and this is altogether consistent with freedom.*b —But how is such an end possible? That is the question now. For the fact that the concept of a thing is possible (contains no contradiction) is not yet sufficient ground for assuming the possibility of the thing itself (the objective reality of the concept).

II.

EXPOSITION OF THE CONCEPT OF AN END WHICH IS AT THE SAME TIME A DUTY

We can conceive the relation of end and duty in two ways: we can begin with the end and seek out the *maxim* of dutiful actions, or we can begin with this maxim and seek out the *end* which is also a duty. —*The doctrine of Law* takes the first way. It leaves it to each man's free choice to decide what end he wants to adopt for his action; but it determines *a priori* the maxim of his action, namely, that the freedom of the agent can co-exist with the freedom of every other in accordance with a universal law.

Ethics takes the opposite way. It cannot begin with the ends a man may set for himself and then prescribe, on this basis, the maxim he ought to adopt—that is, his duty. For in that case the grounds of the maxim would be empirical, and such grounds yield no concept of duty, since this concept (the categorical Ought) has its roots in pure reason alone. Consequently, if maxims had to be adopted on the basis of such ends (all of which are self-seeking), we could not really speak of the concept of duty. —Hence in ethics the *concept of duty* will lead to ends, and *maxims* concerning the ends we *ought* to adopt must be established according to moral principles .

Setting aside the question of what sort of end is in itself a duty and how such an end is possible, we have here only to show that a duty of this kind is called a "*duty of virtue*" and why it is called this.

To every duty there corresponds *one* right in the sense of a *moral title* (*facultas moralis generatim*); but only particular kind of duty, *juridical duty*, implies corresponding *rights* of other people to exercise compulsion (*facultas iuridica*). —In the same way, every ethical *obligation* implies the concept of virtue, but not all ethical duties are thereby duties of virtue. Those duties which concern, not so much a certain end (matter, object of choice), but what is merely *formal* in the moral determination of the will (*e.g.* that the due action should also be done *from the motive of duty*), are not duties of virtue. Only an *end which is also a duty* can be called a duty of virtue. For this reason there can be many duties of virtue (and also many different virtues), while there is only one formal element of moral choice (one virtuous attitude of will), which is, however, valid for all actions.

What essentially distinguishes a duty of virtue from a juridical duty is the fact that external compulsion to a juridical duty is morally possible, whereas a duty of virtue is based only on free self-constraint. —For finite *holy* beings (who can never be tempted to transgress duty) there is no doctrine of virtue but merely a doctrine of morality, since morality is an autonomy of practical reason while virtue is also an *autocracy* of practical reason. Virtue contains, in other words, consciousness of the *power* to master one's inclinations when they rebel against the law—a consciousness which, though not immediately given, is yet rightly deduced from the moral categorical imperative. Thus human morality in its highest stages can still be nothing more than virtue, not even if it were entirely pure (quite free from the influence of any motive other than duty), as when it is often personi-fied poetically in the *Sage*, as an ideal (to which we must continually approximate).

But virtue cannot be defined and valued as a mere *aptitude* or (as the prize-essay of Cochius the court-chap-lain, puts it) a long-standing *habit* of morally good actions, acquired by practice. For unless this aptitude results from considered, firm, and continually purified principles, then, like any other mechanism of technically-practical reason, it is neither armed for all situations nor adequately insured against the changes that new tempta-tions could bring about.

Note

Virtue (= + a) is opposed to *negative lack of virtue* (moral weakness = 0) as its *logical opposite* (*contradicto-rie oppositum*); but it is opposed to vice (= -a) as its *real opposite* (*contrarie s. realiter oppositum*). And it is not only unnecessary but even improper to ask whether great *crimes* might not evidence more strength of soul than do great *virtues*. For by strength of soul we mean the strength of resolution in a man as a being endowed with freedom—hence his strength in so far as he is in control of himself (in his senses) and so in the *state of health* proper to a man. But great crimes are paroxysms, the sight of which makes a man shudder if he is sound of soul. The question would therefore come to something like this: whether a man in a fit of madness could have more physical strength than when he is sane. And we can admit this without attributing more strength of soul to him, if by soul we mean the life principle of man in the free use of his powers; for since a madman's strength, having its source merely in the force of inclinations which *weaken* his reason, manifests no strength of soul, the above question would amount to much the same thing as whether a man could show more strength when he is sick than when he is healthy. This we can straightway deny, since health consists in the balance of all man's bodily powers and sickness is a weakening in the system of these powers; and it is only by reference to this system that we can judge absolute health.

III.

ON THE GROUND FOR CONCEIVING AN END WHICH IS AT THE SAME TIME A DUTY

An *end* is an *object* of free choice, the thought of which determines the power of choice to an action by which the object is produced. Every action, therefore, has its end; and since no one can have an end without *himself* making the object of choice into an end, it follows that the adoption of any end of action whatsoever is an act of *freedom* on the agent's part, not an operation of *nature*. But if this act which determines an end is a practical principle that prescribes the end itself (and therefore commands unconditionally), not the means (and so not conditionally), it is a categorical imperative of pure practical reason. It is, therefore, an imperative which connects a *concept of duty* with that of an end as such.

Now there must be such an end and a categorical imperative corresponding to it. For since there are free actions there must also be ends to which, as their object, these actions are directed. But among these ends there must also be some that are at the same time (that is, by their concept) duties. —For were there no such ends, then all ends would be valid for practical reason only as means to other ends; and since there can be no action without an end, a *categorical* imperative would be impossible. And this would do away with all moral philosophy.

Thus we are not speaking here of the ends man sets for himself according to the sensuous impulses of his nature, but of the objects of free choice under its laws—objects man *ought to adopt* as ends. The study of the former type of ends can be called the technical (subjective) doctrine of ends: it is really the pragmatic doctrine of ends, comprising the rules of prudence in the choice of one's ends. The study of the latter type of ends, however, must be called the moral (objective) doctrine of ends. But this distinction is superfluous here, since the very concept of moral philosophy already distinguishes it clearly from the doctrine of nature (in this case anthropology) by the fact that anthropology is based on empirical principles, while the moral doctrine of ends, which treats of duties, is based on principles given *a priori* in pure practical reason.

IV.
WHAT ENDS ARE ALSO DUTIES?

They are *one's own perfection* and the *happiness of others*.

We cannot interchange perfection and happiness here. In other words, *one's own happiness* and the *perfection of other men* cannot be made into obligatory ends of the same person.

Since every man (by virtue of his *natural* impulse) has *his own happiness* as his end, it would be contradictory to consider this an obligatory end. What we will inevitably and spontaneously does not come under the concept of *duty*, which is *necessitation* to an end we adopt reluctantly. Hence it is contradictory to say that we are *under obligation* to promote our own happiness to the best of our ability.

In the same way, it is contradictory to say that I make another person's *perfection* my end and consider myself obligated to promote this. For the *perfection* of another man, as a person, consists precisely in *his own* power to adopt his end in accordance with his own concept of duty; and it is self-contradictory to demand that I do (make it my duty to do so) what only the other person himself can do.

V.

CLASSIFICATION OF THESE TWO CONCEPTS
A. One's Own Perfection

The word "*perfection*" is open to many misinterpretations. Perfection is sometimes understood as a concept belonging to transcendental philosophy—the concept of the *totality* of the manifold which, taken together, constitutes a thing. Then again, in so far as it be longs to *teleology* it is taken to mean the adequacy of a thing's qualities to an *end*. Perfection in the first sense could be called *quantitative* (material) perfection: in the second, *qualitative* (formal) perfection. The quantitative perfection of a thing can be only one (for the totality of what belongs to a thing is one). But one thing can have a number of qualitative perfections, and it is really qualitative perfection that we are discussing here.

When we say that man has a duty to take as his end the perfection characteristic of man as such (of humanity, really), we must locate perfection in what man can bring into being by his actions, not in the mere gifts he receives from nature; for otherwise it would not be a duty to make perfection an end. This duty must therefore be the *cultivation* of one's *powers* (or natural capacities), the highest of which is *understanding*, the power of concepts and so too of those concepts that belong to duty. At the same time this duty includes the cultivation of one's *will* (moral attitude) to fulfill every duty as such. 1) Man has a duty of striving to raise himself from the crude state of his nature, from his animality (*quoad actum*) and to realize ever more fully in himself the humanity by which he alone is capable of setting ends: it is his duty to diminish his ignorance by education and to correct his errors. And it is not merely technically-practical reason that *counsels* him to acquire skill as a means to his further aims (of art [*Kunst*]): morally-practical reason *commands* it absolutely and makes this end his duty, that he may be worthy of the humanity in him. 2) Man has a duty of cultivating his *will* to the purest attitude of virtue, in which the law is the motive as well as the norm for his actions and he obeys it from duty. This is the duty of striving for inner morally-practical perfection. Since this perfection is a feeling of the influence which the legislative will within man exercises on his power of acting in accordance with this will, it is called *moral feeling*—a special sense (*sensus moralis*), as it were. It is true that moral sense is often misused in a visionary way, as if (like Socrates' genius) it could precede or even dispense with reason's judgment. Yet it is a moral perfection, by which one makes each particular obligatory end one's object.

B. The Happiness of Others

By a tendency of his nature man inevitably wants and seeks his own happiness, *i.e.* contentment with his state along with the assurance that it will last; and for this reason one's own happiness is not an obligatory end.

—Some people, however, invent a distinction between moral happiness, which they define as contentment with our own person and moral conduct and so with what we *do*, and natural happiness, which is satisfaction with what nature bestows and so with what we *enjoy* as a gift from without. (I refrain here from censuring a misuse of the word "happiness" which already involves a contradiction.) It must therefore be noted that the feeling of moral happiness belongs only under the heading of perfection; for the man who is said to be happy in the mere consciousness of his integrity already possesses the perfection defined there as the end which it is also his duty to have.

When it comes to my pursuit of happiness as an obligatory end, this must therefore be the happiness of *other* men, *whose* (permissible) *ends I thus make my own ends as well.* It is for them to decide what things they consider elements in their happiness; but I am entitled to refuse some of these things if I disagree with their judgments, so long as the other has no right to demand a thing from me as his due. But time and again an alleged *obligation* to attend to my own (natural) happiness is set up in competition with this end, and my natural and merely subjective end is thus made a duty (an obligatory end). Since this is used as a specious objection to the division of duties made above (in IV), it needs to be set right.

Adversity, pain, and want are great temptations to transgress one's duty. So it might seem that prosperity, strength, health, and well-being in general, which check the influence of these, could also be considered obligatory ends which make up the duty of promoting *one's own* happiness, and not merely the happiness of others. —But then the end is not the agent's happiness but his morality, and happiness is merely a means for removing obstacles to his morality—a *permissible* means, since no one has a right to demand that I sacrifice my own ends if these are not immoral. To seek prosperity for its own sake is no direct duty, but it can well be an indirect duty: the duty of warding off poverty as a great temptation to vice. But then it is not my happiness but the preservation of my moral integrity that is my end and also my duty.

VI.

ETHICS DOES NOT GIVE LAWS FOR *Actions* (*Ius* DOES THAT),
BUT ONLY FOR *Maxims* OF ACTIONS

The concept of duty stands in immediate relation to a *law* (even if we abstract from all ends, as its matter). We have already indicated how, in that case, the formal principle of duty is contained in the categorical imperative: "So act that the maxim of your action could become a universal law." Ethics adds only that this principle is to be conceived as the law of *your own will* and not of will in general, which could also be the will of another. In the latter case the law would prescribe a juridical duty, which lies outside the sphere of ethics. —Maxims are here regarded as subjective principles which merely *qualify* for giving universal law, and the requirement that they so qualify is only a negative principle; not to come into conflict with a law as such. —How then can there be, beyond this principle, a law for the maxims of actions?

Only the concept of an obligatory *end*, a concept that belongs exclusively to ethics, establishes a law for the maxims of actions by subordinating the subjective end (which everyone has) to the objective end (which everyone ought to adopt as his own). The imperative: "You ought to make this or that (*e.g.* the happiness of another) your end" is concerned with the matter of choice (an object). Now no free action is possible unless the agent also intends an end (which is the matter of choice). Hence, when there is an obligatory end, the maxim of the action, in so far as the action is a means to the end, need only qualify for a possible giving of universal law. As opposed to this, it is the obligatory end that can make it a law to have such a maxim, since for the maxim itself the mere possibility of harmonizing with a giving of universal law is already sufficient.

For the maxims of actions can be *arbitrary*, and come only under the formal principle of action, the limiting condition that they qualify for giving universal law. A *law*, however, does away with this arbitrary element in actions, and by this it is distinguished from *counsels* (which seek to know merely the most appropriate means to an end).

VII.

ETHICAL DUTIES ARE OF *Wide* OBLIGATION, WHEREAS JURIDICAL
DUTIES ARE OF *Narrow* OBLIGATION

This proposition follows from the preceding one; for if the law can prescribe only the maxim of actions, not actions themselves, this indicates that it leaves a playroom (*latitudo*) for free choice in following (observing) the law, *i.e.* that the law cannot specify precisely what and how much one's actions should do toward the obligatory end. —But a wide duty is not to be taken as a permission to make exceptions to the maxim of actions, but only as a permission to limit one maxim of duty by another (*e.g.* love of one's neighbor in general by love of one's parents)—a permission that actually widens the field for the practice of virtue. —As the duty is wider, so man's obligation to action is more imperfect; but the closer to *narrow* duty (Law) he brings the maxim of observing this duty (in his attitude of will), so much the more perfect is his virtuous action.

Imperfect duties, accordingly, are only *duties of virtue*. To fulfill them is *merit* (*meritum* = +a); but to transgress them is not so much *guilt* (*demeritum* = -a) as rather mere *lack of* moral *worth* (= o), unless the agent makes it his principle not to submit to these duties. The strength of one's resolution, in the first case, is properly called only *virtue* (*virtus*); one's weakness, in the second case, is not so much *vice* (*vitium*) as rather mere *want of virtue*, lack of moral strength (*defectus moralis*). (As the word *Tugend* [virtue] comes from *taugen* [to be fit for], so *Untugend* [lack of virtue] comes from *zu nichts taugen* [to be worthless].) Every action contrary to duty is called a *transgression* (*peccatum*). It is when an intentional transgression has been adopted as a basic principle that it is properly called *vice* (*vitium*).

Although the conformity of actions with Law (being a law-abiding man) is not meritorious, the conformity with Law of the maxim of such actions regarded as duties, i.e. reverence for Law, is *meritorious*. For by this we make the right of humanity, or also the rights of men, our *end* and widen our concept of duty beyond the notion of what is *due* (*officium debiti*), since another can demand by right that my actions conform with the law, but not that the law be also the motive for my actions. The same holds true of the universal ethical command: do your duty from the motive of duty. To establish and quicken this attitude in oneself is, again, *meritorious*; for it goes beyond the law of duty for actions and makes the law in itself the motive also.

Hence these duties, too, are of wide obligation. With regard to wide obligation there is present a subjective principle that brings its ethical *reward*—a principle which, to assimilate the concepts of wide and narrow obligation, we might call the principle of receptiveness to this reward in accordance with the law of virtue. The reward in question is a moral pleasure which is more than mere contentment with oneself (this can be merely negative) and which is celebrated in the saying that by this consciousness virtue is its own reward.

If this merit is a man's merit in relation to other men for promoting their natural and so universally recognized end (for making their happiness his own), it could be called *sweet* merit; for consciousness of it produces a moral gratification in which men are prone to *revel* by sympathetic feeling. But *bitter* merit, which comes from promoting the true welfare of others even when they fail to recognize it as such (when they are unthankful and unappreciative), usually has no such reaction. All that it produces is *contentment* with oneself. But in this case the merit would be still greater.

---

*a Yet if a man looks at himself objectively—under the aspect of *humanity* in his own person, as his pure practical reason determines him to do—he finds that, *as a moral being*, he is also holy enough to transgress the inner law *reluctantly*, for there is no man so depraved as not to feel an opposition to this transgression and an abhorrence of himself on account of which he has to constrain himself [to violate the law].—Now it is impossible to explain the phenomenon that at this parting of the ways (where the beautiful fable pictures Hercules between virtue and sensual pleasure) man shows more propensity to listen to his inclinations than to the law. For we can explain what happens only by deriving the event from a cause in accordance with laws of nature, and in trying to explain the act of choice we would not be thinking of it as free. —But it is this mutual and opposing self-constraint and the inevitability of it that makes known the inexplicable property of *freedom* itself.

*b The less a man can be compelled by natural means and the more he can be constrained morally (through the mere thought of the law), so much the more free he is. —Suppose, for example, a man so firm of purpose and strong of soul that he cannot be dissuaded from a pleasure he intends to have, no matter how others may reason with him about the harm he will do himself by it. If such a man gives up his plan immediately, though reluctantly, at the thought it would cause him to omit one of his duties as an official or neglect a sick father, he proves his freedom in the highest degree by being unable to resist the call of duty.

THE CRITIQUE OF JUDGEMENT

PART 1
CRITIQUE OF AESTHETIC JUDGEMENT

FIRST SECTION
ANALYTIC OF AESTHETIC JUDGEMENT

FIRST BOOK
ANALYTIC OF THE BEAUTIFUL

FIRST MOMENT
OF THE JUDGEMENT OF TASTE[1]: MOMENT OF QUALITY

§.1
The judgement of taste is aesthetic.

If we wish to discern whether anything is beautiful or not, we do not refer the representation of it to the Object by means of understanding with a view to cognition, but by means of the imagination (acting perhaps in conjunction with understanding) we refer the representation to the Subject and its feeling of pleasure or displeasure. The judgement of taste, therefore, is not a cognitive judgement, and so not logical, but is aesthetic—which means that it is one whose determining ground *cannot be other than subjective*. Every reference of representation is capable of being objective, even that of sensations (in which case it signifies the real in an empirical representation). The one exception to this is the feeling of pleasure or displeasure. This denotes nothing in the object, but is a feeling which the Subject has of itself and of the manner in which it is affected by the representation.

To apprehend a regular and appropriate building with one's cognitive faculties, be the mode of representation clear or confused, is quite a different thing from being conscious of this representation with an accompanying sensation of delight. Here the representation is referred wholly to the Subject, and what is more to its feeling of life—under the name of the feeling of pleasure or displeasure—and this forms the basis of a quite separate faculty of discriminating and estimating, that contributes nothing to knowledge. All it does is to compare the given representation in the Subject with the entire faculty of representations of which the mind is conscious in the feeling of its state. Given representations in a judgement may be empirical, and so aesthetic; but the judgement which is pronounced by their means is logical, provided it refers them to the Object. Conversely, be the given representations even rational, but referred in a judgement solely to the Subject (to its feeling), they are always to that extent aesthetic.

§.2

*The delight which determines the judgement of taste
is independent of all interest.*

The delight which we connect with the representation of the real existence of an object is called interest.
Such a delight, therefore, always involves a reference to
the faculty of desire, either as its determining ground, or
else as necessarily implicated with its determining
ground. Now, where the question is whether something
is beautiful, we do not want to know, whether we, or
any one else, are, or even could be, concerned in the
real existence of the thing, but rather what estimate we
form of it on mere contemplation (intuition or reflection).
If any one asks me whether I consider that the palace I
see before me is beautiful, I may, perhaps, reply that I do
not care for things of that sort that are merely made to be
gaped at. Or I may reply in the same strain as that
Iroquois *sachem* who said that nothing in Paris pleased
him better than the eating houses. I may even go a step
further and inveigh with the vigour of a *Rousseau* against
the vanity of the great who spend the sweat of the people on such superfluous things. Or, in fine, I may quite
easily persuade myself that if I found myself on an unin-
habited island, without hope of ever again coming
among men, and could conjure such a palace into existence with a mere wish, I should still not trouble to do
so, so long as I had a hut there that was comfortable
enough for me. All this may be admitted and approved;
only it is not the point now at issue. All one wants to
know is whether the mere representation of the object is
to my liking, no matter how indifferent I may be to the
real existence of the object of this representation. It is
quite plain that in order to say that the object is *beautiful*, and to show that I have taste, everything turns on the

meaning which I can give to this representation, and not on any factor which makes me dependent on the real existence of the object. Every one must allow that a judgement on the beautiful which is tinged with the slightest interest, is very partial and not a pure judgement of taste. One must not be in the least prepossessed in favour of the real existence of the thing, but must preserve complete indifference in this respect, in order to play the part of judge in matters of taste.

This proposition, which is of the utmost importance, cannot be better explained than by contrasting the pure disinterested[2] delight which appears in the judgement of taste with that allied to an interest—especially if we can also assure ourselves that there are no other kinds of interest beyond those presently to be mentioned.

§.3
Delight IN THE AGREEABLE *is coupled with interest.*
That is AGREEABLE *which the senses find pleasing in sensation.*

This at once affords a convenient opportunity for condemning and directing particular attention to a prevalent confusion of the double meaning of which the word 'sensation' is capable. All delight (as is said or thought) is itself sensation (of a pleasure). Consequently everything that pleases, and for the very reason that it pleases, is agreeable—and according to its different degrees, or its relations to other agreeable sensations, is attractive, charming, delicious, enjoyable, &c. But if this is conceded, then impressions of sense, which determine inclination, or principles of reason, which determine the will, or mere contemplated forms of intuition, which determine judgement, are all on a par in everything relevant to their effect upon the feeling of pleasure, for this would be

agreeableness in the sensation of one's state; and since, in
the last resort, all the elaborate work of our faculties must
issue in and unite in the practical as its goal, we could
credit our faculties with no other appreciation of things
and the worth of things, than that consisting in the gratification which they promise. How this is attained is in the
end immaterial; and, as the choice of the means is here
the only thing that can make a difference, men might
indeed blame one another for folly or imprudence, but
never for baseness or wickedness; for they are all, each
according to his own way of looking at things, pursuing
one goal, which for each is the gratification in question.

When a modification of the feeling of pleasure or
displeasure is termed sensation, this expression is given
quite a different meaning to that which it bears when I
call the representation of a thing (through sense as a
receptivity pertaining to the faculty of knowledge) sensation. For in the latter case the representation is referred
to the Object, but in the former it is referred solely to the
Subject and is not available for any cognition, not even
for that by which the Subject *cognizes* itself.

Now in the above definition the word sensation is
used to denote an objective representation of sense; and,
to avoid continually running the risk of misinterpretation,
we shall call that which must always remain purely subjective, and is absolutely incapable of forming a representation of an object, by the familiar name of feeling.
The green colour of the meadows belongs to *objective*
sensation, as the perception of an object of sense; but its
agreeableness to *subjective* sensation, by which no object
is represented: i.e. to feeling, through which the object is
regarded as a Object of delight (which involves no cognition of the object).

Now, that a judgement on an object by which its

agreeableness is affirmed, expresses an interest in it, is evident from the fact that through sensation it provokes a desire for similar objects, consequently the delight pre-supposes, not the simple judgement about it, but the bearing its real existence has upon my state so far as affected by such an Object. Hence we do not merely say of the agreeable that it *pleases*, but that it *gratifies*. I do not accord it a simple approval, but inclination is aroused by it, and where agreeableness is of the liveliest type a judgement on the character of the Object is so entirely out of place, that those who are always intent only on enjoyment (for that is the word used to denote intensity of gratification) would fain dispense with all judgement.

§.4
Delight IN THE GOOD *is coupled with interest.*

THAT is *good* which by means of reason commends itself by its mere concept. We call that *good for something* (useful) which only pleases as a means; but that which pleases on its own account we call *good in itself.* In both cases the concept of an end is implied, and con-sequently the relation of reason to (to at least possible) willing, and thus a delight in the *existence* of an Object or action, i.e. some interest or other.

To deem something good, I must always know what sort of a thing the object is intended to be, i.e. I must have a concept of it. That is not necessary to enable me to see beauty in a thing. Flowers, free patterns, lines aim-lessly intertwining—technically termed foliage,—have no signification, depend upon no definite concept, and yet please. Delight in the beautiful must depend upon the reflection on an object precursory to some (not definitely determined) concept. It is thus also differentiated from the agreeable, which rests entirely upon sensation.

In many cases, no doubt, the agreeable and the good seem convertible terms. Thus it is commonly said that all (especially lasting) gratification is of itself good; which is almost equivalent to saying that to be permanently agreeable and to be good are identical. But it is readily apparent that this is merely a vicious confusion of words, for the concepts appropriate to these expressions are far from interchangeable. The agreeable, which, as such, represents the object solely in relation to sense, must in the first instance be brought under principles of reason through the concept of an end, to be, as an object of will, called good. But that the reference to delight is wholly different where what gratifies is at the same time called *good*, is evident from the fact that with the good the question always is whether it is mediately or immediately good, i.e. useful or good in itself; whereas with the agreeable this point can never arise, since the word always means what pleases immediately—and it is just the same with what I call beautiful.

Even in everyday parlance a distinction is drawn between the agreeable and the good. We do not scruple to say of a dish that stimulates the palate with spices and other condiments that it is agreeable—owning all the while that it is not good: because, while it immediately *satisfies* the senses, it is mediately displeasing, i.e. in the eye of reason that looks ahead to the consequences. Even in our estimate of health this same distinction may be traced. To all that possess it, it is immediately agreeable—at least negatively, i.e. as remoteness of all bodily pains. But, if we are to say that it is good, we must further apply to reason to direct it to ends, that is, we must regard it as a state that puts us in a congenial mood for all we have to do. Finally, in respect of happiness every one believes that the greatest aggregate of the pleasure of life, taking duration as well as number into account, merits the name of a true, nay even of the highest, good. But reason sets its face against this too. Agreeableness is enjoyment. But if this is a ll that we are bent on, it would be foolish to be scrupulous about the means that procure it for us—whether it be obtained passively by the bounty of nature or actively and by the work of our own hands. But that there is any intrinsic worth in the real existence of a man who merely lives for *enjoyment*, however busy he may be in this respect, even when in so doing he serves others—all equally with himself intent only on enjoyment—as an excellent means to that one end, and does so, moreover, because through sympathy he shares all their gratifications,—this is a view to which reason will never let itself be brought round. Only by what a man does heedless of enjoyment, in complete freedom and independently of what he can procure passively from the hand of nature, does he give to his existence, as the real existence of a person, an absolute worth. Happiness, with all its plethora of pleasures, is far from being an unconditioned good.[3]

But, despite all this difference between the agreeable and the good, they both agree in being invariably coupled with an interest in their object. This is true, not alone of the agreeable, §.3, and of the mediately good, i.e. the useful, which pleases as a means to some pleasure, but also of that which is good absolutely and from every point of view, namely the moral good which carries with it the highest interest. For the good is the Object of will, i.e. of a rationally determined faculty of desire. But to will something, and to take a delight in its existence, i.e. to take an interest in it, are identical.

---

1 The definition of taste here relied upon is that it is the faculty of estimating the beautiful. But the discovery of what is required for calling an object beautiful must be reserved for the analysis of judgements of taste. In my search for the moments to which attention is paid by this judgement in its reflection, I have followed the guidance of the logical functions of judging (for a judgement of taste always involves a reference to understanding). I have brought the moment of quality first under review, because this is what the aesthetic judgement on the beautiful looks to in the first instance.

2 A judgement upon an object of our delight may be wholly *disinterested* but withal very *interesting*, i.e. it relies on no interest, but it produces one. Of this kind are all pure moral judgements. But, of themselves, judgements of taste do not even set up any interest whatsoever. Only in society is it *interesting* to have taste—a point which will be explained in the sequel.

3 An obligation to enjoyment is a patent absurdity. And the same, then, must also be said of a supposed obligation to actions that have merely enjoyment for their aim, no matter how spiritually this enjoyment may be refined in thought (or embellished), and even if it be a mystical, so-called heavenly, enjoyment.

Religion Within the Limits of Reason Alone

tr. Theodore M. Greene and
Hoyt H. Hudson. New York:
Harper and Row, 1960

(pp. 40–49)

GENERAL OBSERVATION

Concerning the Restoration to its Power of the Original Predisposition to Good

Man *himself* must make or have made himself into whatever, in a moral sense, whether good or evil, he is or is to become. Either condition must be an effect of his free choice; for otherwise he could not be held responsible for it and could therefore be *morally* neither good nor evil. When it is said, Man is created good, this can mean nothing more than: He is created *for good* and the original *predisposition* in man is good; not that, thereby, he is already actually good, but rather that he brings it about that he becomes good or evil, according to whether he adopts or does not adopt into his maxim the incentives which this predisposition carries with it ([an act] which must be left wholly to his own free choice).

Granted that some supernatural cooperation may be necessary to his becoming good, or to his becoming better,
yet, whether this cooperation consists merely in the
abatement of hindrances or indeed in positive assistance,
man must first make himself worthy to receive it, and
must *lay hold* of this aid (which is no small matter)—that
is he must adopt this positive increase of power into his
maxim, for only thus can good be imputed to him and he
be known as a good man.

How is it possible for a naturally evil man to make
himself a good man wholly surpasses our comprehension; for how can a bad tree bring forth good fruit? But
since, by our previous acknowledgement, an originally
good tree (good in predisposition) did bring forth evil
fruit,*1 and since the lapse from good into evil (when
one remembers that this originates in freedom) is no
more comprehensible than the re-ascent from evil to
good, the possibility of this last cannot be impugned. For
despite the fall, the injunction that we *ought* to become
better men resounds unabatedly in our souls; hence this
must be within our power, even though what *we* are able
to do is in itself inadequate and though we thereby only
render ourselves susceptible of higher, and for us
inscrutable, assistance. It must indeed be presupposed
throughout that a seed of goodness still remains in its
entire purity, incapable of being extirpated or corrupted;
and this seed certainly cannot be self-love*2 which, when
taken as the principle of all our maxims, is the very
source of evil.

The restoration of the original predisposition to
good in us is therefore not the acquiring of a *lost* incentive for good, for the incentive which consists in respect
for the moral law we have never been able to lose, and
were such a thing possible, we could never get it again.

Hence the restoration is but the establishment of the *purity* of this law as the supreme ground of all our maxims, whereby it is not merely associated with other incentives, and certainly is not subordinated to any such (to inclinations) as its conditions, but instead must be adopted, in its entire purity, as an incentive *adequate* in itself for the determination of the will. Original goodness is the *holiness of maxims* in doing one's duty, merely for duty's sake. The man who adopts this purity into his maxim is indeed not yet holy by reason of his act (for there is a great gap between the maxim and the deed). Still he is upon the road of endless progress towards holiness. When the firm resolve to do one's duty has become habitual, it is also called the *virtue* of conformity to law; such conformity is virtue's *empirical character* (*virtus phænomenon*). Virtue here has as its steadfast maxim conduct *conforming to law*; and it matters not whence come the incentives required by the will for such conduct. Virtue in this sense is won *little by little* and, for some men, requires long practice (in observance of the law) during which the individual passes from a tendency to vice, through gradual reformation of his conduct and strengthening of his maxims, to an opposite tendency. For this to come to pass a *change of heart* is not necessary, but only a *change of practices*. A man accounts himself virtuous if he feels that he is confirmed in maxims of obedience to his duty, though these do not spring from the highest ground of all maxims, namely, from duty itself. The immoderate person, for instance, turns to temperance for the sake of health, the liar to honesty for the sake of reputation, the unjust man to civic righteousness for the sake of peace or profit, and so on—all in conformity with the precious principle of happiness. But if a man is to become not merely *legally*, but *morally*, a

good man (pleasing to God), that is, a man endowed
with virtue in its intelligible character (*virtus noumenon*)
and one who, knowing something to be his duty,
requires no incentive other than this representation of
duty itself, *this* cannot be brought about through gradual
reformation so long as the basis of the maxims remains
impure, but must be effected through a *revolution* in the
man's disposition (a going over to the maxim of holiness
of the disposition). He can become a new man only by a
kind of rebirth, as it were a new creation (John III, 5;
compare also Genesis I, 2), and a change of heart.

But if a man is corrupt in the very ground of his
maxims, how can he possibly bring about this revolution
by his own powers and of himself become a good man?
Yet duty bids us do this, and duty demands nothing of us
which we cannot do. There is no reconciliation possible
here except by saying that man is under the necessity of,
and is therefore capable of, a revolution in his cast of
mind, but only of a gradual reform in his sensuous
nature (which places obstacles in the way of the former).
That is, if a man reverses, by a single unchangeable decision, that highest ground of his maxims where by he was
an evil man (and thus puts on the new man), he is, so far
as his principle and cast of mind are concerned, a subject
susceptible of goodness, but only in continuous labor
and growth is he a good man. That is, he can hope in
the light of that purity of the principle which he has
adopted as the supreme maxim of his will, and of its sta-
bility, to find himself upon the good (though strait) path
of continual *progress* from bad to better. For Him who
penetrates to the intelligible ground of the heart (the
ground of all maxims of the will) and for whom this
unending progress is a unity, *i.e.*, for God, this amounts
to his being actually a good man (pleasing to Him); and,

thus viewed, this change can be regarded as a revolution. But in the judgment of men, who can appraise themselves and the strength of their maxims only by the ascendancy which they win over their sensuous nature in time, this change must be regarded as nothing but an ever-during struggle toward the better, hence as a gradual reformation of the propensity to evil, the perverted cast of mind.

From this it follows that man's moral growth of necessity begins not in the improvement of his practices but rather in the transforming of his cast of mind and in the grounding of a character; though customarily man goes about the matter otherwise and fights against any vices one by one, leaving undisturbed their common root. And yet even the man of greatest limitations is capable of being impressed by respect for an action conforming to duty—a respect which is the greater the more he isolates it, in thought, from other incentives which, through self-love, might influence the maxim of conduct. Even children are capable of detecting the smallest admixture of improper incentives; for an action thus motivated at once loses, in their eyes, all moral worth. This predisposition to goodness is cultivated in no better way than by adducing the actual *example* of good men (of that which concerns their conformity to law) and by allowing young students of morals to judge the impurity of various maxims on the basis of the actual incentives motivating the conduct of these good men. The predisposition is thus gradually transformed into a cast of mind, and *duty*, for its own sake, begins to have a noticeable importance in their hearts. But to teach a pupil to *admire* virtuous actions, however great the sacrifice these may have entailed, is not in harmony with preserving his feeling for moral goodness. For be a man never so virtuous, all the goodness he can ever perform is still his simple duty; and to do his duty is nothing more than to do what is in the common moral order and hence in no way deserving of wonder. Such wonder is rather a lowering of our feeling for duty, as if to act in obedience to it were something extraordinary and meritorious.

Yet there is one thing in our soul which we cannot cease from regarding with the highest wonder, when we view it properly, and for which admiration is not only legitimate but even exalting, and that is the original moral predisposition itself in us. What is it in us (we can ask ourselves) whereby we, beings ever dependent upon nature through so many needs, are at the same time raised so far above these needs by an idea of an original predisposition (in us) that we count them all as nothing, and ourselves as unworthy of existence, if we cater to their satisfaction (though this alone can make life worth desiring) in opposition to the law—a law by virtue of which our reason commands us potently, yet without making either promises or threats? The force of this question every man, even one of the meanest capacity, must feel most deeply—every man, that is, who previously has been taught the holiness which inheres in the idea of duty but who has not yet advanced to an inquiry into the concept of freedom, which first and foremost emerges from this law:*3 and the very incomprehensibility of this predisposition, which announces a divine origin, acts perforce upon the spirit even to the point of exaltation, and strengthens it for whatever sacrifice a man's respect for his duty may demand of him. More frequently to excite in man this feeling of the sublimity of his moral destiny is especially commendable as a method of awakening moral sentiments. For to do so works directly against the innate propensity to invert the incentives in the maxims of our will and toward the re-establishment in the human heart, in the form of an unconditioned respect for the law as the ultimate condition upon which maxims are to be adopted, of the original moral order among the incentives, and so of the predisposition to good in all its purity.

But does not this restoration through one's own exertions directly contradict the postulate of the innate corruption of man which un fits him for all good? Yes, to be sure, as far as the conceivability, *i.e.*, our *insight* into the possibility, of such a restoration is concerned. This is true of everything which is to be regarded as an event in time (as change), and to that extent as necessary under the laws of nature, while at the same time its opposite is to be represented as possible through freedom under moral laws. Yet the postulate in question is not opposed to the possibility of this restoration itself. For when the moral law commands that we *ought* now to be better men, it follows inevitably that we must *be able* to be better men. The postulate of innate evil is of no use whatever in moral *dogmatics*, for the precepts of the latter carry with them the same duties and continue in identical force whether or not there is in us an innate tendency toward transgression. But in moral *discipline* this postulate has more to say, though no more than this: that in the moral development of the predisposition to good implanted in us, we cannot start from an innocence natural to us but must begin with the assumption of a wickedness of the will in adopting its maxims contrary to the original moral predisposition; and, since this propensity [to evil] is inextirpable, we must begin with the incessant counter-action against it. Since this leads only to a progress endlessly continuing, from bad to better, it follows that the conversion of the disposition of a bad man into that of a good one is to be found in the change of the highest inward ground of the adoption of all his maxims, conformable to the moral law, so far as this new ground (the new heart) is now itself unchangeable. Man cannot attain naturally to assurance concerning such a revolution, however, either by immediate consciousness or through the evidence furnished by the life which he has hitherto led; for the deeps of the heart (the subjective first ground of his maxims) are inscrutable to him. Yet he must be able to *hope* through his *own* efforts to reach the road that leads thither, and which is pointed out to him by a fundamentally improved disposition, because he ought to become a good man and is adjudged *morally* good only by virtue of that which can be imputed to him as performed by himself.

Against this expectation of self-improvement, reason, which is by nature averse to the labor of moral reconstruction, now summons, under the pretext of natural incapacity, all sorts of ignoble religious ideas (among which belongs the false ascription to God Himself of the principle of happiness as the chief condition of His commandments). All religions, however, can be divided into those which are *endeavors to win favor* (mere worship) and *moral* religions, *i.e.*, religions of *good life-conduct*. In the first, man flatters himself by believing either that God can make him eternally happy (through remission of his sins) without his having *to become a better man*, or else, if this seems to him impossible, that *God* can certainly *make him a better man* without his having to do anything more than to *ask* for it. Yet since, in the eyes of a Being who sees all, to ask is no more than to *wish*, this would really involve doing nothing at all; for were improvement to be achieved simply by a wish, every man would be good. But in the moral religion (and of all the public religions which have ever existed, the Christian alone is moral) it is a basic principle that each must do as much as lies in his power to become a better man, and that only when he has not buried his inborn talent (Luke XIX, 12-16) but has made use of his original predisposition to good in order to become a better man, can he hope that what is not within his power will be supplied through cooperation from above. Nor is it absolutely necessary for a man to know wherein this cooperation consists; indeed, it is perhaps inevitable that, were the way it occurs revealed at a given time, different people would at some other time form different concepts of it, and that with entire sincerity. Even here the principle is valid: "It is not essential, and hence not even necessary, for every one to know what God does or has done for his salvation;" but it is essential to know *what man himself must do* in order to become worthy of this assistance.

This General Observation is the first of four which are appended, one to each Book of this work, and which might bear the titles, (1) Works of Grace, (2) Miracles, (3) Mysteries, and (4) Means of Grace. These matters are, as it were, *parerga* to religion within the limits of pure reason; they do not belong within it but border upon it. Reason, conscious of her inability to satisfy her moral need, extends herself to high-flown ideas capable of supplying this lack, without, however, appropriating these ideas as an extension of her domain. Reason does not dispute the possibility or the reality of the objects of these ideas; she simply cannot adopt them into her maxims of thought and action. She even holds that, if in the inscrutable realm of the supernatural there is something more than she can explain to herself, which may yet be necessary as a complement to her moral insufficiency, this will be, even though unknown, available to her good will. Reason believes this with a faith which (with respect to the possibility of this supernatural complement) might be called *reflective*; for *dogmatic* faith, which proclaims itself as a form of *knowledge*, appears to her dishonest or presumptuous. To remove the difficulties, then, in the way of that which (for moral practice) stands firm in and for itself, is merely a by-work (*parergon*), when these difficulties have reference to transcendent questions. As regards the damage resulting from these *morally*-transcendent ideas, when we seek to introduce them into religion, the consequences, listed in the order of the four classes named above, are: (1) [corresponding] to imagined inward experience (works of grace), [the consequence is] *fanaticism*; (2) to alleged external experience (miracles), *superstition*; (3) to a supposed enlightening of the understanding with regard to the supernatural (mysteries), *illumination*, the illusion of the "adepts"; (4) to hazardous attempts to operate upon the supernatural (means of grace), *thaumaturgy*—sheer aberrations of a reason going beyond its proper limits and that too for a purpose fancied to be moral (pleasing to God).

But touching that which especially concerns this General Observation to Book One of the present treatise, the calling to our assistance of *works of grace* is one of these aberrations and cannot be adopted into the *maxims* of reason, if she is to remain within her limits; as indeed can nothing of the supernatural, simply because in this realm all use of reason ceases. For it is impossible to find a way to define these things *theoretically* ([showing] that they are works of grace and not inner natural effects) because our use of the concept of cause and effect cannot be extended beyond matters of experience, and hence beyond nature. Moreover, even the hypothesis of a *practical* application of this idea is wholly self-contradictory. For the employment of this idea would presuppose a rule concerning the good which (for a particular end) we ourselves must *do* in order to accomplish something, whereas to await a work of grace means exactly the opposite, namely, that the good (the morally good) is not our deed but the deed of another being, and that we therefore can *achieve* it only by *doing nothing*, which contradicts itself. Hence we can admit a work of grace as something incomprehensible, but we cannot adopt it into our maxims either for theoretical or for practical use.

---

*1 The tree, good in predisposition, is not yet good in actuality, for were it so, it could certainly not bring forth bad fruit. Only when a man had adopted into his maxim the incentive planted in him of allegiance to the moral law is he to be called a good man (or the tree a thoroughly good tree.)

*2 Words which can be taken in two entirely different meanings frequently delay for a long time the reaching of a conviction even on the clearest of grounds. Like *love* in general, so also can *self-love* be divided into love of *good will* and love of *good pleasure* (*benevolentiae et complacentiae*), and both (as is self-evident) must be rational. To adopt the former into one's maxim is natural (for who will not wish to have it always go well with him?); it is also rational so far as, on the one hand, that end is chosen which can accord with the greatest and most abiding welfare, and, on the other, the fittest means are chosen [to secure] each of the components of happiness. Here reason holds but the place of a handmaid to natural inclination; the maxim adopted on such grounds has absolutely no reference to morality. Let this maxim, however, be made the unconditional principle of the will, and it is the source of an incalculably great antagonism to morality.

A rational love of *good pleasure in oneself* can be understood in either of two ways: first, that we are well pleased with ourselves with respect to those maxims already mentioned which aim at the gratification of natural inclination (so far as that end is attained through following those maxims); and then it is identical with love as good will toward oneself: one takes pleasure in oneself, just as a merchant whose business speculations turn out well rejoices in his good discernment regarding the maxims he used in these transactions. In the second sense, the maxim of self-love as *unqualified good pleasure* in oneself (not dependent upon success or failure as consequences of conduct) would be the inner principle of such a contentment as is possible to us only on condition that our maxims are subordinated to the moral law. No man who is not indifferent to morality can take pleasure in himself, can indeed escape a bitter dissatisfaction with himself, when he is conscious of maxims which do not agree with the moral law in him. One might call that a *rational self-love* which prevents any adulteration of the incentives of the will by other causes of happiness such as come from the consequences of one's actions (under the name of a thereby attainable happiness). Since, however, this denotes an unconditional respect for the law, why needlessly render difficult the clear understanding of the principle by using the term *rational self-love*, when the use of the term *moral self-love* is restricted to this very condition, thus going around in a circle? (For only he can love himself in a moral fashion who knows that it is his maxim to make reverence for the law the highest incentive of his will.) By our *nature* as beings dependent upon circumstances of sensibility, we crave happiness first and unconditionally. Yet by this same nature of ours (if we wish in general so to term that which is innate), as beings endowed with reason and freedom, this happiness is far from being first, nor indeed is it unconditionally an object of our maxims; rather this object is *worthiness to be happy*, *i.e.*, the agreement of all our maxims with the moral law. That this is objectively the condition whereby alone the wish for happiness can square with legislative reason—therein consists the whole precept of morality; and the moral cast of mind consists in the disposition to harbor no wish except on these terms.

*3 The concept of the freedom of the will does not precede the consciousness of the moral law in us but is deduced from the determinability of our will by the law as an unconditional command. Of this we can soon be convinced by asking ourselves whether we are certainly and immediately conscious of power to overcome, by a firm revolve, every incentive, however great, to transgression (*Phalaris licet imperet, ut sis falsus, et admoto dicet periuria tauro* [Juvenal, *Satires* VIII, 81-82: "though Phalaris himself should command you to be false and should bring up his bull and dictate perjuries."]). Everyone will have to admit that he *does not know* whether, were such a situation to arise, he would not be shaken in his resolution. Still, duty commands him unconditionally: he *ought* to remain true to his resolve; and thence he rightly *concludes* that he must *be able* to do so, and that his will is therefore free. Those who fallaciously represent this inscrutable property as quite comprehensible create an illusion by means of the word *determinism* (the thesis that the will is determined by inner self-sufficient grounds) as though the difficulty consisted in reconciling this with freedom—after which all never occurs to one; whereas what we wish to understand, and never shall understand, is how *predeterminism*, according to which voluntary actions, as events, have their determining grounds in *antecedent time* (which, with what happened in it, is no longer within our power), can be consistent with freedom, according to which the act as well as its opposite must be within the power of the subject at the moment of its taking place.

To reconcile the concept of freedom with the idea of God as a *necessary* Being raises no difficulty at all: for freedom consists not in the contingency of the act (that it is determined by no grounds whatever), *i.e.*, not in indeterminism (that God must be equally capable of doing good or evil, if His actions are to be called free), but rather in absolute spontaneity. Such spontaneity is endangered only by predeterminism, where the determining ground of the act is in *antecedent* time, with the result that, the act being now no longer in *my* power but in the hands of nature, I am irresistibly determined; but since in God no temporal sequence is possible, this difficulty vanishes.

Index